ALCOHOL AND HOMICIDE

SUNY SERIES IN VIOLENCE
DAVID LUCKENBILL, EDITOR

ALCOHOL AND HOMICIDE

A Deadly Combination of Two American Traditions

ROBERT NASH PARKER
WITH
LINDA-ANNE REBHUN

STATE UNIVERSITY OF NEW YORK PRESS

Published by
State University of New York Press, Albany

© 1995 State University of New York

For information, address State University of New York
Press, State University Plaza, Albany, N.Y., 12246

Production by E. Moore
Marketing by Dana Yanulavich

Library of Congress Cataloging-in-Publication Data

Parker, Robert Nash.
    Alcohol and homicide : a deadly combination of two American
traditions / Robert Nash Parker, Linda-Anne Rebhun.
        p.   cm. — (SUNY series in violence)
    Includes bibliographical references and index.
    ISBN 0-7914-2463-4 (HC : alk. paper). — ISBN 0-7914-2464-2 (PB :
alk. paper)
    1. Alcoholism and crime—United States—History. 2. Alcoholism
and crime—United States. 3. Liquor laws—United States.
4. Homicide—United States—Prevention. I. Rebhun, Linda-Anne.
II. Title. III. Series.
HV5053.P37 1995
364.1′532′0973—dc20   94-26255
                                                              CIP

Contents

FIGURES AND TABLES

FIGURES

TABLES

The research reported in this book has its traceable origins in the early fall of 1988, when I was faced with a deadline for a proposal for a faculty developmental assignment leave at the University of Iowa, where I had been teaching since 1984. After giving up some credit in years of full-time teaching experience at Rutgers University and the University of Akron when I came to Iowa, I would be eligible for the Iowa version of a sabbatical leave in the 1989-90 academic year. My partner, Cecilia L. Ridgeway, was also eligible for such a leave in the same year, a happy circumstance that led us to consider leaving Iowa City for the year and taking up temporary residence somewhere else. We hoped we could find someplace with better weather—although we both to this day have fond memories of our time in Iowa City, of the quality people, the top scholars, the bright students, and the really good friends we made there. Cecilia had previously done research and published with a colleague at Stanford, and was quickly able to secure the promise of a National Institute of Mental Health (NIMH) fellowship as part of a training program being conducted at the Stanford sociology department, which decided for us that the San Francisco Bay area was to be our destination.

Developmental assignments, like many sabbatical programs available for faculty in American universities, provided for either full salary for one semester, or one-half salary for two semesters. Even though the NIMH stipend was not equal to the other one-half of a salary, the possibility of this fellowship at Stanford meant that between us we would have nearly three-fourths of our usual salaries combined, sufficient for temporary residence even in northern

California, where some necessities, like housing, are more expensive than they are in Iowa. Things would improve for us during the developmental leave year if I could also secure a similar fellowship or supplement.

In this atmosphere of need, I had been thinking as well about what kind of proposal I would write for the developmental assignment. The University of Iowa does not grant every request for such leaves, although a faculty member can usually get such a leave with the support of their department and a proposal that seems likely to enhance their teaching and research activities upon their return to campus. In discussing these issues with friends over dinner one night, Mac Marshall, anthropology professor and accomplished alcohol researcher, suggested I contact two national research centers in Berkeley, the Alcohol Research Group, directed at that time by Robin Room, and the Prevention Research Center, directed by Harold D. Holder, for they had a training program that might be the solution to the other almost one-half of my salary. I did so, and received a warm and welcome reception from Drs. Holder and Room, and was awarded a one-year fellowship for 1989-90.

In speaking to Room and Holder before writing my proposal to the training grant and to the University of Iowa, it became evident that although there was more interest in the field of alcohol research in the question of the relationship between alcohol and homicide (and violence more generally), there was not much more in the way of a body of research on this relationship in alcohol research as compared to criminology and sociology, where there was almost nothing. I was referred to James J. Collins' collection, *Drinking and Crime* (1981), which was revealing and enlightening. Collins (1981: 290) himself argued that Wolfgang's (1958) pioneering study, which was at that time more than twenty years old, was the exemplary study of the homicide alcohol relationship. As that research was by that time more than thirty years old, and there had been, to my knowledge, nothing more recent published on this relationship, I was encouraged but cautious. My dissertation advisor, Joel Smith, used to warn us at Duke in his design seminar, just because there is a lack of research in an area does not always mean there is an opportunity—it could be there are some good theoretical or methodological reasons why there is little in the way of existing literature.

There had been some theoretical work, represented particularly by the work of Pernanen (1976; 1981; this was before his 1991 study was published), but this work had been general and at a high level of abstraction. Pernanen's theoretical arguments had a great deal of influence on this work and the formulation of the problem. What really seemed to be needed was more specific theoretical development, in which theories of violent criminality, of which there are no shortage in the literature, be logically analyzed in terms of the role that alcohol might play in the genesis of violence in general and homicide in particular. This was the project that I proposed for the National Institute on Alcohol Abuse and Alcoholism (NIAAA) postdoctoral fellowship, which was supported by the Alcohol Research Group and the Prevention Research Center. Because my approach (and the approach generally taken in criminology) to homicide causation was macrosocial in orientation, Holder, Room, and their colleagues thought that the Prevention Research Center would be a better fit for me than the Alcohol Research Group, which has traditionally had a more epidemiological approach to alcohol research.

The year in California was a productive one, with the theoretical development and the beginnings of a number of empirical papers resulting. It seemed clear that the result of this would ultimately be a book-length manuscript. After I had read, studied, attended the postdoctoral training seminar, and talked with researchers at the two centers in Berkeley, and was convinced that such a project could be accomplished, I began to circulate a proposal for this book. Happily, in the fall of 1990, SUNY Press and Rosalie Robertson, then acquisitions editor, offered me a contract. As I had never contemplated a book before, I was pleased that someone else thought that the enterprise had merit, and I signed the contract quickly.

I continued then to pursue the development of the larger project, both theoretical (at first) and empirical (later in the postdoctoral year). I had submitted a proposal to the National Science Foundation (NSF) in 1989, which was funded in 1990 by a joint effort of the sociology (Murray Webster, director) and the law and social sciences programs (Felice Levine, director). I could begin to see possible fruition down the road. I began to present versions of the theoretical arguments at the American Sociological Association and American Society of Criminology meetings. With NSF support, I began to build the empirical base of this research program. I returned to Iowa in the fall of 1990, and continued to write the early versions of the theory development (Parker, 1993a). I began to analyze the empirical data I had been collecting and had obtained from colleagues Paul Gruenewald at the Prevention Research Center and Terry Miethe than at Virginia Polytechnic Institute (VPI) (Parker, 1991, 1992a, 1992b). A happy circumstance then occurred—Cecilia Ridgeway obtained an offer from Stanford, and eventually I received an offer from the Prevention Research Center for a full-time position. Moving back to California and to the Prevention Research Center provided me with the resources and support for this project, even after the National Science Foundation (NSF) grant came to its conclusion. The Prevention Research Center national center grant from NIAAA made this effort and this product possible.

WHAT THIS STUDY IS *NOT* ABOUT

No study, even book-length, can cover every topic that every reader wishes to be included, and the current effort is no exception. In fact, I have often been urged, usually in anonymous reviews, to *simplify* my approach, to be less comprehensive in the inclusiveness of my research, an issue with which I have dealt elsewhere (Parker, 1994b). A number of people, experts and the general public included, have responded to my brief descriptions of this research program offered at meetings, parties, and on airplanes by asking why focus on alcohol, and why not focus on other things that those individuals perceive as more important or more powerful explanations of homicide. The rest of this book should provide a detailed set of answers to the first question. As for the second set of questions, I will briefly respond to the two most common ones: why not study illegal drugs and homicide, and why not study guns and homicide? My answers to these questions here in no way undermines the legitimacy of someone, now or in the future, who wants to study the relationship between these things and homicide; I may even do such research myself in the future! I do think there are good reasons to study alcohol and homicide, as I have already indicated and will discuss by way of theories, hypotheses, and empirical data in this book. I do think there are good reasons not to study drugs or guns and homicide before or in addition to alcohol, given the development process I have described here.

Drugs and Homicide

During the 1980s a great deal of public attention, media coverage, and government resources were devoted to drugs and the self-styled war on drugs. There is no doubt that illegal drugs are a major problem in American society, and that violence is linked to illegal drugs. A closer examination reveals, however, that the connection between violence and drugs is, in the main, fundamentally different from the link between alcohol and violence. With few exceptions, the violence associated with illegal drugs, especially homicide, is associated with the *distribution* and *sale* of drugs, not with the *use* of drugs. Even in cases where drug users commit crimes to finance drug purchases, these crimes are more often property in nature, and when users commit violent crimes, they are not usually under the influence of drugs. On the other hand, the violence that is associated with alcohol is almost always committed when either the offender, the victim, or both have used alcohol prior to the event. Thus alcohol is much more proximate to the event, and therefore the inference that alcohol has something to do with the event is more credible.

Further evidence from ethnographic and detailed accounts of homicides (Samuels, 1976; Wilbanks, 1984) suggests that in a significant number, perhaps a majority, of the murders associated with illegal drug distribution and sales are in fact alcohol-related, in that one or both participants had consumed alcohol prior to the event, making these homicides alcohol-related, not illegal drug-related. Finally, it is well known that groups of more or less organized young men have fought over territory in the cities of the United States long before the illegal drug trade became a major activity of youth gangs. Although other factors (firearms) may have exacerbated the problem, the argument that this violence is driven solely by illegal drugs is hard to sustain.

Finally, it should be pointed out that despite the problem that illegal drug use represents in the United States, alcohol consumption is dramatically more widespread and much more integrated into everyday life. This makes the study of the alcohol and homicide relationship much more pressing and important than that between illegal drug use and homicide.

Guns and Homicide

The situation with the firearm and homicide relationship is different from that for illegal drugs and homicide. It seems reasonable to believe that the increase in the number and character of weapons available on the street in cities has had a significant effect on the homicide rate. But the current knowledge base goes little beyond belief, because the research needed to address this connection has not been done. This is because the data are hard to come by. We know how many gun homicides there are, and it is possible to know how many gun suicides, robberies, assaults, and even accidents there are (see the pioneering work of Philip J. Cook (1981, 1991). We also know, from the recent work of Colin Loftin, David McDowall, and their colleagues what happens when laws are passed at the state or local level that are designed to restrict access to guns or to further deter their illegal use in certain situations (Loftin and McDowall, 1981, 1984; Loftin et al., 1992). However, there is no direct measure of the number of guns by locality, and therefore we cannot know the net impact of actual gun density on homicide rates, net of other factors. I simply do not feel that the proxies we have developed warrant inclusion in a study such as this, with the further caveat that the theories I examine in this research do not specify the role of firearms. Of course, these theories do not specify a role for alcohol, but the work that led to this project involved deducing the connections. A similar effort would be needed to draw out the implications that firearm density, even if it could be measured directly, would have on these theories of homicide.

Last of all, this is not a microlevel study of alcohol and homicide. I am not concerned with predicting the likelihood that an individual who consumes some alcohol will engage in or be the victim of a violent act. Both the research literatures that are combined in this book—alcohol research and criminology—have traditionally studied their respective dependent variables from a macrosocial point of view. This is in part because it is at the macro level where the interesting variation is—that is, very, very, very few people in the adult United States population ever commit a homicide, but cities and states vary a great deal in terms of the rate of homicide. It is also in part because the prevention of homicide—that is, in terms of legal and other public policy initiatives that could or might be used to address the homicide problem—are macro in nature—for example, new sanctions for homicide or for using a gun in a criminal act, gun control laws, alcohol regulations concerning distribution, taxation, minimum age of purchase, and so on. Any study has limitations, and the macrostudy presented here is no exception.

A thorough reading of this work will, I believe, appropriately reveal the strengths and weaknesses of the approach I have taken. As for the strengths and weaknesses of a microapproach to the study of alcohol and crime, I have dealt with this issue at length elsewhere (Parker, 1994b). None of this is intended to devalue high quality research on illegal drugs, guns, and homicide, either micro or macro, but rather to reveal to the reader of this work my own views and justifications for the book as you will find it.

ACKNOWLEDGMENTS

No research of any kind, let alone of the scope required to produce a book, can be accomplished without the support and assistance of many, many individuals and institutions. I will mention those that I feel were most helpful and supportive. I want to make it clear to the many others who will not be mentioned that I am sincerely grateful for the ways in which they helped me to complete this book.

First of all, I would like to gratefully acknowledge the agencies, organizations, and institutions that provided financial support for the project, in terms of both direct material support and salary support for me and L.-A. Rebhun while we worked on the research and writing summarized here. First of all, the University of Iowa supported this project through the granting of a developmental assignment leave, in 1989-90. I would particularly like to thank Edward J. Lawler (now of Cornell University), who was chair of the department of sociology, Mary Smith, departmental administrator, and Gerhard Loewenberg, than dean, College of Liberal Arts. The University of California School of Public Health, Berkeley, provided support via the joint Alcohol Research Group/Prevention Research Center Training Grant, #T32-AA07240, from the National Institute of Alcohol Abuse and Alcoholism, during 1989-90. The training grant was directed by Robin Room and Harold D. Holder, directors of the two research centers. The National Science Foundation, sociology and law and social sciences programs, provided support for this effort via a grant to me, "Homicide in Urban America, 1950-1980," #SES-9000474, 9/90-2/93. Murray Webster and Felice Levine were directors of the respective programs.

xviii   Acknowledgments

Finally, I should like to gratefully acknowledge the support of the National Institute of Alcohol Abuse and Alcoholism for the National Research Center grants they have awarded to the Prevention Research Center, #AA-06282. Although NIAAA did not directly support this project, Harold D. Holder, in his role as director of the Prevention Research Center, adopted this project as a priority, and provided both encouragement and resources to a degree that would have been impossible without the center grant from NIAAA. Both he and Robert F. Saltz, associate director of the Prevention Research Center, provided the impetus for research on violence and alcohol to become a major focus at the center. My joining them full-time in 1991 was greatly facilitated by the fact that Bob Saltz, along with Michael Hennessy, whose position I filled after Hennessy departed for the Centers for Disease Control and Prevention in Atlanta, had already begun development on a violence and alcohol component for the center grant renewal application, thus creating a legitimate position in the center for the topic of alcohol and violence. Thus I am very grateful to Bob Saltz, whose encouragement and interest in the alcohol and violence relationship has had a major impact on this book, as well as the entire program of alcohol and violence research that I have developed at the Prevention Research Center.

I would also like to acknowledge my other colleagues at the Prevention Research Center, including Joel Grube, Genevieve Ames, and Paul Gruenewald. They have provided me with supportive work environment, encouragement, and support for the development of violence as an additional area at the Prevention Research Center. And they have provided me with friendship, a scarce good that is so often missing in the high-pressure, competitive work places of today. These people have been uniformly encouraging and supportive of this project, and have earned my gratitude and my respect for this and other examples of the way in which they have all worked to create an atmosphere most conducive to giving each member of the group the opportunity and the resources to succeed at the highest level.

Among these colleagues, I would like to especially acknowledge the support and friendship of Maria Luisa Alaniz, my collaborator on one of the extensions to the program of research described here, and a person who has been a consistent source of support and enthusiasm throughout the latter half of this project. Maria's genuine sense of excitement about this book has been so helpful that sometimes when I was discouraged, as any author can often get during the difficult trail that leads from prospectus to finished manuscript, her enthusiasm and excitement for the book and its goals was contagious for me, and helped me renew my own sense of excitement and commitment. Along these same lines, I would also like to thank Magdalena Avila and Angela Gallegos, whose excitement and sense of joy over seeing the competed manuscript provided me with a sense of success that helped to overcome the natural anticlimatic reaction that any author has upon completion of a manuscript.

Despite all the contributions of the people I have mentioned so far, there are three others whose support and contributions to this project literally made this project possible, and it is no cliché to state that without their support, this book would not have been possible. First and foremost, I should like to acknowledge the support, encouragement, affection, and companionship of my friend and partner, Cecilia L. Ridgeway. I cannot adequately describe the kind of support, encouragement, motivation, and friendship she has provided, and the positive kind of environment that she and I have been able to create for each other during the seven years that we have been together. Cecilia never doubted that I could complete this book, even when I was finding it difficult to imagine, and finding it hard, within the context of making a transition from full-time teaching and research in an academic setting to full-time research in a nonacademic setting, to find the time for this project. Cecilia also sacrificed my companionship on many evenings and weekends during the past four years, when I retreated to the study to work on the research and writing for this book. I know that she felt the loss of my companionship, as I felt the loss as well, but she never begrudged the time I needed to complete the book, and she was unwavering in her support. If I were to dedicate this work to a single person, it would be to Cecilia L. Ridgeway.

The second person for whom I reserve special appreciation is my coauthor on chapter 1, Linda-Anne Rebhun. Linda-Anne sought me out during her first year as a postdoctoral fellow in the NIAAA training grant described previously, because she had some interest in the alcohol and violence relationship. As we discussed our interests, it became apparent that the place where they overlapped was in the area of the historical origins of the alcohol and violence relationship, particularly in the nineteenth century in the United States.

We both felt that the current situation, in which alcohol and violence are linked at an almost unconscious cultural level, should be traceable to pre-Civil War patterns and practices that had become ingrained in the cultural psyche of the United States, and reinforced by the western frontier and the role it played in the development of the American ethos of individualism and self-sufficiency. I initially hired Linda-Anne to do some abstracting of primary and secondary sources dealing with alcohol and violence from this period, but as her interest and involvement grew, it became obvious that I should offer her the chance to coauthor the first chapter with me so that she could help me to write the exciting historical material her research had uncovered. I view Linda-Anne's contribution to this project as an essential one, as it helps to explain and document why alcohol and violence are as closely linked as they are today. The remainder of the book would be much less compelling if Linda-Anne's clear and concisely written material on the historical origins of this relationship were to be removed from the book. I am responsible for the rest of the manuscript, however, so that any criticisms applied to chapters 2 through 6 should be directed solely toward me. I would like to acknowledge Linda-Anne Rebhun's contribution to this book, and to say how much I enjoyed working with her on it. She has an intensity that is rare among scholars of any age, and her analytic and writing skills are extraordinary. She also has a keen and sarcastic wit, which I appreciate very much, perhaps more than she realizes; I find that she often makes the amusing and ironic remark that I wish I had thought of in the situations we often find ourselves in as we work together at the Prevention Research Center.

The third person I would like to give special acknowledgment to for his fundamental role in the genesis of this work is Terry Miethe, professor and chair, department of criminal justice, University of Nevada-Las Vegas. Terry has been a great friend and colleague in sociology and criminology circles for many years, and he has been a major supporter of this project. He helped in a number of ways, most important of which was as a soundingboard for the development of many of the important design features and theoretical ideas that are utilized here. Terry also generously supplied longitudinal data files, which I was about to duplicate in preparation for this project. This gave me the ability to merge my data files with his, and saved a great deal of time and effort on my part, time and effort that I was able to redirect into other aspects of this project. Terry would often shrug off his contribution as no problem, but I have built similar data bases in the past, and I know the amount of effort that such data bases can absorb. I am extremely grateful to Terry for this and his general encouragement and enthusiasm for having me go after the "big" study, when I was sometimes hesitant and wanted to take a safer, more conventional route.

I would like to briefly mention a number of other people, organizations, and institutions to whom I feel beholden for the support, direct and indirect, that they lent to this enterprise. Mimi Hill and Jane Lowe, who both worked at the Prevention Research Center at various times over the past few years, were talented and diligent research assistants in this project, and were essential in the location and entry of the alcohol outlet density data used here. Randi Cartmill, who is currently my research assistant at the Prevention Research Center, created the index and offered editorial assistance that I greatly appreciated. Monique Adam, administrator, Prevention Research Center, provided the major editorial assistance out of friendship and interest in the work I was doing, and I am very grateful indeed to her. Anita Martin, graphics whiz and word processing expert, offered advice and shared expertise that enabled me to complete the graphics and word processing of the manuscript with increased efficiency and ease. Judy Gerson, professor of sociology at Rutgers-New Brunswick, Mac Marshall, professor of anthropology, University of Iowa, and Andrew Abbott, professor of sociology at the University of Chicago, all offered support, friendship, and key reactions, sometimes in situations that the three of them may not even remember, but which I remember well, and which provided me with a new perspective or conceptual approach to an aspect of the argument and analysis found here. I would also like to thank some of my colleagues at the Alcohol Research Group in Berkeley, the sister research center to the Prevention Research Center. Their presence in the same part of Berkeley surely gives us the greatest concentration for world-class research on the social and behavioral aspects of alcohol on the planet. I would like to mention Robin Room, now of the Addiction Research Foundation, Toronto, Constance Weisner, senior scientist, and Cheryl Sherpitel, senior scientist, for their encouragement and collegiality over the years.

I should like to gratefully acknowledge four institutions that offered me a forum for presenting the main ideas and a version of the analysis during the spring of 1991 when this project was in a critical stage: the sociology department at the University of Arizona, especially Travis Hirschi and Paula England; the University of Colorado and the Institute for Behavioral Sciences, especially Delbert Elliot and Kirk Williams; the sociology department at the University of New Mexico, especially Gary LaFree; and Carnegie-Mellon University, especially Jacqueline Cohen and Alfred Blumstein. I should also like to thank the American Society of Criminology and the American Sociological Association, for the opportunity to present various and sundry versions of the ideas and analyses presented here over the last five years. These opportunities to present papers and get some reaction from colleagues was very helpful in shaping the final product. I have often heard people say that presenting at these meetings does not do anything for one's work or career, but I would like to offer my experience and this book as a contrary example.

Finally, I would like to thank the State University of New York Press for believing in this project and offering me a contract at a crucial time, and for their help in getting this from idea to manuscript to published book; Christine Worden, acquisitions editor, and Rosalie Robertson, her predecessor (now at the University of Wisconsin Press), were very helpful and encouraging. I would also like to thank my family, especially my brother, Bill Parker II and his family, whose almost finished family room proved to be an inspiration for some of the important writing during a beautiful New England fall day; my parents, Bill and Connie Parker, who provided me with the opportunity and resources to become a researcher and who put up with my lugging around large cases full of book-related materials and computer equipment every time I visited them during the last four years as I made slow and not always steady progress toward completion of this book; and my sister Nancy Reynolds and her family for encouraging me to work on what they thought was an important problem in their community. I would also like to thank Jaqueline Ridgeway, Cecilia Ridgeway's mother, for similarly tolerating a lot of computer equipment, research materials, and my disappearances into her study to work on this project, plus the bill for those phone calls I made to various computers for analysis and references that she never would give me.

To all of these and others, I owe the existence of this book. I take full responsibility for the work, however, as it appropriately reflects my unique and sometimes quite quirky point of view. I benefited greatly from the wisdom of others, but in the end I made my own stand, whether wise or foolish or both. I am ultimately thankful to have had the opportunity to do this research and write this book, as the opportunity itself has been a great journey of self-discovery and self-actualization. If our work can at least improve us, and have a chance to improve others, then I consider it more than worthwhile to have worked.

Chapter 1

ALCOHOL AND HOMICIDE
AMERICAN STYLE

The beginning of recorded human history is replete with stories of homicide and alcohol. Both Greco-Roman and Judeo-Christian cultural histories place major emphasis on accounts of murder among the founding mythologies and legends. Chinese, African, and the native cultures of the Americas also contain such accounts, and the common recurrence of these homicidal incidents undoubtedly reflects the fact that homicide has been a part of the human behavioral repertoire for at least several thousand years. There is also substantial evidence that alcohol has been part of human material culture for thousands of years as well. The Sumerians brewed beer at least five thousand years ago, the founding Western cultures of the Mediterranean region worshiped gods devoted to alcohol, and the Aztecs of Central America drank pulque, an alcoholic beverage of fermented maguey juice, in religious ceremonies and in old age (Austin, 1985; Madsen and Madsen, 1969).

The link, however, between violence and alcohol has not been prominent in most cultures, either historic or current, industrialized or preindustrialized. It seems that the United States is unique in the establishment of a cultural system in which these two traditional elements are brought together. Studies of the place of alcohol in nonindustrialized cultures indicate that alcohol is linked to a wide variety of behaviors, but not very often to violence (Marshall, 1979). Even in the United States during the late eighteenth and nineteenth century, the period during which, as we shall argue below, the critical elements of the alcohol and violence link in American culture were being formed, concern about the negative impact of alcohol abuse was more focused on breakdowns in the "social order" in general—for example, family, work, political participation, and so on—than on violence per se (Rorabaugh, 1979). Despite the fact that both alcohol and violence have been the subjects of major research efforts in the last fifty years, the recognition of ùhe strong cultural and behavioral connection between them has not been reflected in a major research effort. This is not to say that some individual researchers and research projects have not recognized this connection or have not highlighted its importance, but rather to point out that neither of the fields of alcohol research or criminology has included the study of alcohol and violence as an important area of focus. The origins of this lack of attention are beyond the scope of this discussion, except to suggest that the reasons are numerous and interconnected, involving issues such as the politics of research funding, disciplinary boundaries, and the emphasis on applied versus basic research in the social sciences.

Although there have been significant efforts in alcohol research to study the impact of this drug on violence—Pernanen (1991), Steele and Josephs (1990), Kantor and Straus (1987), Leonard (1989), Goodman et al. (1985) being some of the more recent examples—evidence of the lack of focus on this topic is not hard to find. The National Institute of Alcohol Abuse and Alcoholism (NIAAA) released a request for proposals on alcohol and violence in 1993, in which the rationale for increased attention to this link is stated as:

> Nevertheless, understanding of the mechanisms by which alcohol influences violent behavior has been limited. . . . Theoretical explanations of alcohol-induced violence have tended to focus on only one aspect of the problem, and in turn, efforts to prevent such violence have been limited. (p. 1)

At a conference sponsored by the secretary of health and human services, Dr. Louis Sullivan, material prepared for attendees by the Office of Substance Abuse Prevention (1992) cited the most prominent and important study of alcohol and homicide to date, Marvin Wolfgang's (1958) landmark analysis of homicide patterns in Philadelphia, from which the often cited finding that two-thirds of homicides involve alcohol use by either the victim, the offender, or both originates. However, the citation given to this study was taken from a much more recent publication (National Committee for Injury Prevention and Control, 1989), thus giving the impression that these data were recent. We are certain that the authors of this material had no intention to deceive the conference attendees, but the fact that the exemplary citation on the link between alcohol and homicide is more than thirty-five years old illustrates the lack of attention and scientific progress on this topic (see Collins, 1981:290 for a similar argument).

As far as criminology is concerned, there has also been some attention paid to the alcohol and violence connection (Widom, 1989; Collins, 1981; Fagan, 1990; White et al., 1987; Lindqvist, 1986; Hammock and Richardson, 1993; Parker, 1993a). However, a recent review of homicide research (Parker, 1994a) demonstrates that although Wolfgang's (1958) study spawned a major research program among criminologists on homicide causation, alcohol is almost completely missing from this area of research and from the study of violence causation in general. We would argue that a large part of the problem of theoretical "myopia" noted by the NIAAA program announcement is the lack of attention to the alcohol and violence relationship—both theoretically and empirically—on the part of the discipline within which violence is a topic of major focus—criminology.

Given the undeveloped nature of this area of research, what are the major unanswered questions? First and foremost, the question of whether alcohol is simply associated with homicide or plays a causal role in the generation of homicide, remains largely unaddressed. Two kinds of research are needed to begin to answer this question. Theoretical analysis of alcohol's potential and multiple roles in the social and behavioral processes that lead to homicide needs to be advanced. This is the area where the current research literature is most developed, due in large part to the important work of Pernanen (1976, 1981, 1991). Second, a vast increase in the number and variety of empirical studies in which alcohol and homicide are both measured is needed. As Pernanen (1981) points out, there are relatively few studies that actually measure both of these variables. Many of the ones that do are limited to one time point (Wolfgang, 1958; Parker, 1992b), one not so typical or generalizable place (Pernanen, 1991), or have a very limited set of additional variables available (Welte and Abel, 1989).

Two additional questions will concern us here, questions that are directly subsidiary to the questions of causality versus association, and the only appropriate way to generate answers to these two questions is to advance the two types of research on alcohol and homicide identified here, theoretical and empirical, in that order. If we assume that the "correct" answer to the first question is that alcohol does cause homicide in some fashion, the second question for theoretical analysis is to specify the details of the causal mechanisms that lead from alcohol to homicide. In other words, why does alcohol cause homicide, and how does this occur? Recent theoretical work has made a start in this direction (Fagan, 1990; Parker, 1993a), and that effort will be extended and expanded here. Only by placing the alcohol and homicide relationship in the context of a number of theories of violence causation is it possible to begin to understand how alcohol would relate to the causes identified in the criminological research literature.

In addition, only with some increase in our knowledge of how and why alcohol affects homicide can we begin to intervene. Public policy directed toward violence in general and homicide in particular is outstanding only for its failure. Deterrence theory, especially that which involves the use of the death penalty to deter homicide, has noticeably failed to have any effect on homicide (Smith and Parker, 1980; Bowers, 1984; Bailey and Peterson, 1989; Bailey, 1990). Alcohol control policy, on the other hand, has had some moderate successes in the recent past, in particular with regard to the increases in the minimum drinking age which occurred for the most part during the 1980s and which led to reductions in drinking and driving accidents among youth (O'Malley and Wagenaar, 1991; Saffer and Grossman, 1987). If such a policy could be found to have a similar impact on homicide (Parker, 1991), a new realm of possibilities would be opened with regard to policies designed to reduce homicide in particular and perhaps violence in general.

The third question, following from the first two, depends on placing the hypothesized relationships among alcohol, other causes

of homicide, and homicide itself in empirical models that are sufficiently complex to account for homicide and the many factors that
may cause it. This requires advanced statistical analysis of data that
are sufficiently generalizable, both in space and in time, to warrant
confidence in the evaluations of these hypotheses that will be generated by this exercise. Two sets of empirical data, both longitudinal
and generalizable to the United States as a whole, will be subjected
to analysis with two different if equally complex statistical
approaches, structural equation models, and pooled cross section
time series analysis.

However, before the effort to answer these questions can be
undertaken, the cultural and social origins of the link between violence and alcohol, which we have argued is uniquely American
(referring by this term to United States society explicitly) must be
traced historically, and it is to that task that we now turn.

CULTURAL AND SOCIAL ORIGINS
OF THE ALCOHOL AND VIOLENCE LINK

Alcohol and homicide have not always been so explicitly linked
in the United States as we would assert they are today. We will
argue here that the origins of the link, however, can be traced polit-
ically, socially, and economically to the circumstances and events in
the United States from the late eighteenth century, throughout the
nineteenth century, and into the pre-World War II portion of the
twentieth century. The structural conditions of these times within
which the origins of a connection between alcohol and violence
occurred have for the most part, if not completely, vanished. Once
these conditions provided a socially approved, ideological, and behavioral basis for the connection, alcohol and violence became part of a
cultural and social tradition in United States society, with only
Prohibition posing a partial threat to the established link between
alcohol and violence. We shall have more to say about the relationship between Prohibition and this connection, but at this point it is
important to recognize that neither contemporary reports nor more
recent historical analysis of the time period of interest here, 1750-
1920, focus on this link.

In thinking about the negative effects of alcohol on society
during this period, both types of observers are more likely to be con-

cerned about breakdowns in the social order other than violence: family dissolution, loss of productivity, disease, and anarchy (Rorabaugh, 1979). Only discussions of the latter contain references to violence, although it seems clear that homicide and other forms of interpersonal violence were less central in these analyses than were subversion of the social hierarchy, family neglect, and riots and revolts in response to state action (Mather, 1708; Adams, 1760 [1865]; Hines, 1828; Rorabaugh, 1979:54-55, 190). However, we shall argue that there were a number of specific examples of political violence motivated directly by alcohol, which are much more important for the building of the cultural and social substructure, that led to the establishment of this cultural tradition. The link between alcohol and violence against the state is not that citizens under the influence revolt against tyranny in general, something they would have been reluctant to do if sober, but rather something more complex.

Considering the historical evidence of interpersonal violence, it also seems clear that what evidence there is shows that homicide and other forms of violence were not especially aggravated by increases in alcohol consumption during the nineteenth century. For example, in the United Kingdom, during the height of the expansions of gin production, between 1840 and 1855 (Rorabaugh, 1979:238), records show a significant decline in homicide rates in the city of London (Daly and Wilson, 1988: 276). Despite much contemporary discussion of alcohol and the social order in the United States during the eighteenth and nineteenth centuries, a similar conclusion is warranted, as alcohol consumption declined significantly between 1840 and 1880 (Rorabaugh, 1979: 8), at the same time as violent crime was increasing (Ferdinand, 1967). How can it be that during the time period in which the substructural bases for an alcohol and violence link were forming and developing, there was very little manifestation of this relationship? These features developed slowly during this period and continued to develop into their final form into the twentieth century. Prohibition may have delayed this growth in one sense, that being a temporary reduction in alcohol-induced interpersonal violence, but it also served to further accelerate development of the current form of the relationship because of violent clashes between the state and criminal elements bent on defying Prohibition through smuggling and illegal production of alcohol (Ayers, 1984: 263-64).

However, just as Weber (1898 [1958]) argued about the ancient civilizations of the Mediterranean and capitalism, having the cultural elements for a strong link between alcohol and violence, does not necessarily result in that link being manifested throughout a society. After Prohibition, a major increase in alcohol consumption was needed to bring the alcohol and violence link to the surface. Such an increase began in 1950, peaking in 1980. Although a slight decline has occurred since 1980 (Sparrow et al., 1989), the magnitude of this decline is certainly not sufficient to result in a breakdown of the alcohol and violence link. One purpose of this study is to suggest how public policy might be directed to weaken the link without waiting for this decline, if it continues, to have such an effect.

HISTORICAL ORIGINS OF THE ALCOHOL AND VIOLENCE LINK IN THE UNITED STATES

Patterns of alcohol use, concepts of alcohol abuse, and the relationship between alcohol use and violent behavior have changed over the course of United States history, in response to political, religious, and economic shifts. In addition, the complex relationships among the many ethnic groups that make up the United States population have affected both consumption of alcohol and propensity to violence. Alcohol-related violence has taken the form of individual violence such as brawls in bars, duels of honor, and battles over the production and sale of illegal alcoholic beverages, and collective violence in response to the government's attempts to control alcohol production and sale.

History of Alcohol Consumption and Attitudes in the United States

The concept of alcohol abuse dates from the late eighteenth century in the United States. Before that time, the idea that alcohol was a dangerous, addictive, or harmful substance was not widespread (Levine, 1984: 109). Indeed, early settlers in what was to become the United States saw alcohol as good for health, drinking it at and between meals, and making medicines with it. The Puritans, who dominated among New England colonists, called it "the good creature of God," in recognition of its status as a gift from heaven. Both men and women drank alcohol, especially fermented beverages, daily. And while public drunkenness was a punishable offense, it was considered a moral flaw of the drunken individual, rather than a problem with alcohol itself (Levine 1983: 115-16).

The early settlers drank homemade fermented beverages with their meals, because water was considered dangerous to drink (Earle, 1913: 147) (and given the state of sanitation, it probably was). Milk was not introduced as a drink for adults at meals until the 1630s, and its consumption was largely confined to breakfast (Earle, 1913: 148), leaving beer, ale, hard cider, perry (made from pears), peachy (made from peaches), and other fruit- and grain-based fermented beverages as the main liquids consumed for lunch and supper.

The consolidation of the slave trade in the 1700s, and the resulting boom in plantation-based sugar production, meant that large amounts of molasses became available, and rum was produced in large amounts. Unlike fermented beverages, rum was used mainly at celebrations and as an after-work relaxer in the colonial period (Earle, 1913: 163). Colonists did not define mild inebriation as drunkenness. A rhyme of the time gave the following definition:

> Not drunk is he who from the floor
> can rise again and still drink more
> But drunk is he who prostrate lies
> Without the power to drink or rise.
> (Bridenbaugh, 1971, cited in Levine, 1983: 117)

Puritans saw drunkenness as sinful, because it was a form of sloth, and their religion was strict in its work demands. But although they noticed that fights tended to break out at taverns, they blamed that on the use of taverns as meeting places for gamblers, prostitutes, criminals, unemployed men, and other unsavory characters, rather than on the effects of the alcohol served there. In addition, their theology stressed the importance of free will, and therefore they could not remain true to their religion while positing that alcohol changed people's ability to freely choose their actions (Levine, 1983: 120-22).

This generally positive attitude toward alcohol changed under the pressure of a number of factors, including the increased production of distilled beverages, the decline of Puritanism and rise of Quakerism among colonists, increased ethnic, religious, and economic diversity among colonists, and after the Revolution, the ideas of physicians such as Dr. Benjamin Rush, who saw excessive alcohol consumption as not merely a vice, but a disease.

With the proliferation of distilled beverages and the increased ethnic diversity of new world immigrants, the production, sale, and consumption of alcohol was increasingly important in ethnic tensions among the many groups who made up the fledgling society of the new world, because access to alcohol and patterns of consumption were influenced by ethnic affiliation. Enslaved Africans were prohibited from producing or consuming alcohol except with their owner's permission (Huggins, 1971: 108). In addition, different class and ethnic groups within the white majority had varying patterns of drinking. And alcohol was a major commodity traded between whites and Indians, playing an important role in the fur trade along the western frontier (Hunt, 1983: 34).

Drinking on the Frontier

Today, we think of the far west as the frontier, but until the consolidation of the western territories as states, the frontier was on the western edge of existing states. Writing in 1893, Frederick Jackson Turner described the movement west of the frontier over time:

> The fall line marked the frontier of the seventeenth century; the Alleghenies that of the eighteenth; the Mississippi that of the first quarter of the nineteenth; the Missouri that of the middle of this century (omitting the California movement); and the belt of the Rocky Mountains and the arid tract, the present frontier. (Turner, 1894; cited in Winkler, 1968: 414)

Frontiersmen were even heavier drinkers than colonists, prone to binges in town as respite from hard days and nights working in difficult conditions. And Native Americans soon developed a reputation as heavy, violent drinkers. In fact, from the earliest times of settlement, Native Americans and enslaved Africans were the only groups colonists recognized as stimulated to violence by alcohol (Levine, 1983: 123; Tyrrell, 1982: 490; Walton, 1970: 728).

Native Americans had no traditional fermentation or distillation skills (except for a few tribes south of the 35th north latitude who made fermented beverages) (Heath, 1985: 208) and could only get alcohol from whites, who saw this as an opportunity to open advantageous new markets. Alcohol was traded for furs and access to territory (Hunt, 1983: 34; Winkler, 1968: 429-31). While not all the tribes easily accepted alcohol, others were ravaged by its widespread use (Heath, 1985: 208). Unlike groups that have produced and consumed alcohol for millennia, Native Americans had no social strictures within which to contain their drinking. Combined with the extreme depression accompanying the destruction of their cultures through conquest, these factors led to a pattern of heavy drinking in some tribes, which continued into the twentieth century (Dozier, 1966: 80).

This pattern was also encouraged by white traders who encouraged Native Americans to drink, partly to accustom them to alcohol so that they would trade for it, and partly to inebriate them so that they could be more easily swindled in trading. Traders swapped so-called Indian whiskey for furs and buffalo robes. This concoction was described by one Missouri River trader as follows:

> You take one barrell of Missouri River water, and two gallons of alcohol. Then you add two ounces of strychnine—because strychnine is the greatest stimulant in the world—and three plugs of tobacco to make them sick—an Indian wouldn't figure it was whiskey unless it made him sick—and five bars of soap to give it a head, and a half a pound of red pepper, and then you put in some sagebrush and boil it until it's brown. Strain into a barrell, and you've got your Indian whiskey; that one barrell calls for one buffalo robe and when the Indian got drunk it was two robes. (Abbot and Smith, 1939: 123-24, cited in Winkler, 1968: 430)

Often, Native American drinking was accompanied by quarreling, fighting, and murder. There soon arose a stereotype of the violent "drunken Indian" who would trade anything for more "fire water." As a priest noted in 1750:

> The savages—especially the Illinois, who are the gentlest and most tractable of men—become when intoxicated, madmen and wild beasts. They fall upon one another, stab with their knives, and tear one another. (MacAndrews and Edgerton, 1969: 101-3, cited in Levine, 1983: 123)

Colonists and frontiersmen regarded Native Americans as brutish pagans, and blamed their pattern of drinking on innate sav-

agery. Similarly, slave holding southerners, always fearful of insurrections, argued that drink brought out what they saw as the bestial
nature of the African. Starting in the early 1700s they passed laws
prohibiting sale of alcohol to blacks (Walton, 1970: 729).

However, the evidence is that there were plenty of brawls
among drunken whites in colonial times. It was just that in the
opinion of the colonists, their own behavior had different roots than
the similar behavior of Native Americans and enslaved Africans. By
the nineteenth century, public opinion on the relationship of alcohol
to violence had changed, and whites began to attribute their own
violence to the effects of alcohol (Levine, 1983: 124). This change
reflected not only increasing prosperity as the new country matured
and former immigrants became members of a well-established middle class, but also increasing ethnic diversity among European immigrants, leading established Americans to fear fellow whites as dangerously different.

Although early settlers and frontiersmen did not attribute their
violence to the effects of alcohol, looking back from today's van-
tage point, we can see how alcohol consumption articulated with the
ethnic and class divisions of early American society. While alcohol
itself did not cause the brawls, battles, and insurrections common in
those violent times, it did influence how and where brawls got
started. Its nature as a valuable commodity inspired violence over its
regulation and trade.

Individual Violence: Brawls, Duels, and Battles

Patterns of violence in a society—who fights whom, in which way,
and over what issues—reflect the dynamics of cultural beliefs and
both inter- and intragroup relationships (Gorn, 1985: 18). Fistfights,
pistol duels, lynchings, and beatings have been an integral part of
struggles over ownership of territory, rights to produce and sell
goods, conflicts between ethnic groups, and gender relations in the
United States from colonial times and continuing until today. A
belief in the right of free persons to use violence in defense of their
freedoms, and a self-image as a nation founded on the basis of liberty
play a central role in the United States psyche. In addition,
Americans have resisted attempts to limit the access to alcohol.

Levels and forms of violence have varied in different historical
periods and different regions. Violence was especially strong in the

antebellum south and along the western frontier. The legendary violence of the west has been attributed to its nature as a frontier, yet the similar Canadian and Australian frontiers did not see such brutality. And violence was not confined to the frontier, being so commonplace in the south that some have suggested frontier violence was a result of southerners moving westward through Texas rather than a condition of the frontier itself (Ayers, 1984: 12). Violence in the south can be traced back to the tensions that existed between racial groups in this slavery-based society, and especially among the varying economic classes of whites. Central to the relationship between alcohol and violence in the old south and the western frontier was the concept of male personal honor.

In an honor-based system, personal worth is dependent on the opinions of others (in contrast, a dignity-based system vests worth in the intrinsic value of a human being). This makes honor unstable, because others' opinions are changeable (Gorn, 1985: 39; Ayers, 1984: 12-13). It is maintained through continual demonstration of characteristics considered symbolic of honor and immediate violent response to any perceived insult. An insult unanswered has the potential to change the public opinion on which honor is based, and so it must be obliterated. In the antebellum south, only white men were considered to have honor, and only white women to have virtue. The condition of slavery excluded black men from honor, and meant that black women could not defend their sexual virtue against the advances of their owners.

In the system of male honor that developed in the southern and western United States, the reputation on which honor was based depended on power. The more powerful a man, the more esteem he could command. Some men, like the slave holders and landowners, commanded economic power. For others, behaviors such as drinking, boasting, and fighting, were both symbolic and demonstrative of power. Being very touchy about insults was also honorable, because it marked the difference between a servile slave and a proud free man, since slaves were not permitted to fight or to answer back to insult (Gorn, 1985: 41). And it showed that the man had honor to defend.

Not all white men were honorable. To be honorable, a man had to demonstrate his freedom, self-reliance, and therefore strength, his ability to defend the virtue of his women from other men, and his courage and therefore willingness to defend his reputation to the death if need be. This demonstration could be direct or symbolic.

Symbolic demonstrations of male honor included heavy drinking, brawling, and prodigious boasting.

Throughout the south it was the privilege of white men to engage in duels over honor. Among the upper classes, these took the form of formal pistol duels, with official challenges, seconds, and the ritual of pacing, turning, and shooting. But the lower-class men were famous for their eye-gouging, lip-biting-off, and ear-ripping fisticuffs (Ayers, 1984: 3; Gorn, 1985).

These duels were so popular that Virginia, South Carolina, and North Carolina were all forced to pass laws making a felony out of "premeditated mayhem" defined as cutting out tongues, pulling, gouging, or plucking out eyes, biting or cutting off noses, or stomping upon citizens, in unsuccessful attempts to prevent them (Gorn, 1985: 19). Rough-and-tumble or gouging was a form of fighting in which the combatants went at it with no holds barred, with special attention paid to mutilating the opponent's body parts. Some famous brawlers grew their fingernails long especially to aid in the gouging out of eyes. The fights ended when one or the other combatant was unable to continue, or cried for mercy (Gorn, 1985: 20).

Often these brawls started in bars, and both combatants were inebriated. One contemporary commentator, writing in 1880, stated:

> [One] could hardly fail to be impressed with the prevalence of whiskey-drinking and the frequency of fighting with deadly weapons . . . when the whiskey begins to work, it very often happens that there is a fight between parties having what is locally called "a grudge." (Redfield, 1880, cited in Ayers, 1984: 14)

It would be an error to attribute the popularity of these duels to simple lawlessness. Duels and brawls reflected a combination of economic and interethnic tensions with a strict code of honor in the context of a comparatively weak state. In comparison to the power of the slave-holding landed class, the state had relatively little clout, and legal sanctions against whites of all classes were lenient. In contrast, slavery's coercive mechanisms against drinking, disobedience, and attempted violence by black slaves were harsh (Ayers, 1984: 132-34).

Slavery was a moral anomaly in a country that prided itself on its freedoms. Because blacks as a class were held to be separate from whites and without honor, all whites felt superior to all blacks. But in addition, there was an economic hierarchy among white males, who ranged from the planter classes to the impoverished indentured servants (Ayers, 1984: 26). This led to great tensions among the poorer class of whites, who were eager to show their difference from and superiority to blacks, and frustrated by their exclusion from the upper white classes. For example, the emphasis on mutilation in rough-and-tumble fighting was part of the attempt of lower-class men to distinguish themselves from slaves. Since it was illegal to mutilate slaves, the facial mutilations of the rough-and-tumble fighters served to announce their status as free men who could allow themselves to be mutilated if they so chose (Gorn, 1985: 42).

Class and ethnic tensions found outlet in competitions over who could out-boast, out-lie, out-drink, out-fight, and generally outdo whom. Men also competed to be more generous or convivial than their fellows (Gorn, 1985: 22), often seeing who could buy the most rounds, drink them, and tell the hairiest yarns while being ready to start fighting should the occasion arise. Legendary Mississippi keelboatman Mike Fink, for example, was quoted as saying:

> I'm a salt River roarer! I'm a ring-tailed squeeler! I'm a regular screamer from the old Massassip! Whoop! I'm the very infant that refused his milk before its eyes were open and called out for a bottle of old Rye! I love the women and I'm chockful o' fight! I'm half wild horse and half cock-eyed alligator and the rest o' me is crooked snags an' red-hot snappin' turtle. . . . I can out-run, out-jump, out-shoot, out-brag, out-drink, an' out-fight, rough-an'-tumble, no holts barred, any man on both sides the river from Pittsburg to New Orleans an' back ag'in to St. Louiee! (Blair and Meine, 1933: 105-6, cited in Gorn, 1985: 29)

Alcohol was inextricably integrated into the image of these "brave . . . heavy drinkers, coarse frolickers in moral sties . . . heavy fighters, reckless fellows" (Twain, 1883: 24, cited in Gorn, 1985: 35). It was almost always a lubricant for brawls, either to give the contestants "liquid courage" or because status conflicts were enhanced in the convivial, masculine atmosphere of bars.

An act such as buying a round of drinks for the men at a bar was demonstrative of power, because it showed that the buyer had sufficient resources to pay for the large number of drinks. It also marked the buyer as a leading, generous member of the group of men in the bar. In addition, it was symbolic of status, because not all people in society were permitted to drink or buy drinks. Women and minors, for example, were excluded from bars, and slaves could only drink with their master's permission and could neither buy drinks for nor accept drinks from others (Huggins, 1971: 108). Participating in the buying and consuming of drink rounds was therefore symbolic of membership in the group and equality, and refusing to accept a drink was an insult to the buyer, because it implied that the refuser thought he was superior to the buyer (Gorn, 1985: 40). Given the deadly seriousness with which insult was regarded in the male honor complex, buying and accepting drinks was a highly charged process that could explode in violence at a moment's notice. Any existing tensions between rival groups could be brought to a head by the ritualized offering and refusal of drinks, making bars dangerous places to frequent.

Brawling in bars was not confined to the south and west of the country. In the north, immigrant Irish and Italian workers were thought dangerous for their attributed tendency to drink, gamble, smoke, curse, brawl, engage in mob violence, and subscribe to free-thinking ideas (Dodd, 1978: 515). Here, as in the south, alcohol-related violence reflected ethnic and class tensions.

Brawling and dueling eventually fell out of favor, partly because as the frontier moved further west and finally disappeared, life became less rough-and-ready in general, but also because the Civil War changed ethnic and class relations. The invention of efficient weapons such as rifles and pistols changed the methodology of combat. The ritualized code duello of the upper classes began to seem too ceremoniously cold-blooded (Ayers, 1984: 268), and as the inaccurate, misfiring pistols, which had made it survivable, were replaced by efficient firearms, therefore making it too dangerous.

In addition, the Civil War marked the last major challenge to the power of the federal government over the states, and as power was increasingly centralized, justice was increasingly the responsibility of governments to provide. Private justice in the form of vigilantism, feuds, and brawls was increasingly associated with the lower classes, as the upper and middle classes turned to the law to settle their disputes. Access to state-sponsored police work, courts, and legal protections became an increasingly important marker of class. Today, the complex of hypersensitivity to insult and symbolic demonstration of manhood through drinking, violence, and sexual acting-out is most prevalent among disenfranchised, impoverished, lower-class men (Ayers, 1984: 275) who cannot expect justice in courts and so must carve out their own version of it for themselves.

Collective Violence

Because there is no natural limit to demand for alcohol and because it is consumed with no remainder, it constitutes a perfect commodity, the sales of which are limited only by the purchasing capacity of the buyer (Hunt, 1983: 34). This makes it extraordinarily profitable to produce. Collective violence over regulation and taxation of alcohol production and sale has erupted periodically in United States history. Like personal violence, this collective violence has reflected concerns over the nature and implications of freedom and the association of freedom with honor, as well as racial and ethnic tensions. Like drinking, the production of alcoholic beverages was a white privilege during slavery; most states prohibited both slaves and black freedmen from distilling or selling liquor (Huggins, 1971: 108; Walton, 1970: 729).

In 1791 the colonial congress of the newly independent United States imposed an excise tax on a number of products including distilled spirits in order to replenish the national coffers after the Revolutionary War (Glaser, 1976: 75). Gallons of whiskey produced in the United States were taxed according to their proof, and yearly taxes were imposed on stills as well. In addition, producers were ordered to maintain records of their produce, and all sites relevant to the production and sale of distilled spirits including distilleries, storage areas, taverns, and the like, were ordered to permit government inspection (Klein, 1976: 30-31). This tax was especially bothersome in Pennsylvania, Kentucky, Virginia, and Tennessee, major producers of whiskey (Glaser, 1976: 31). Making grain into whiskey was much more profitable than selling it as cereal; it brought a better price, was more easily transported, and aged rather than spoiled (Klein, 1976: 25). The heavy tax sharply reduced profits; the inspections were seen as unwarranted invasions of privacy.

Because the Revolution was sparked by resistance to British regulation and taxation, residents believed that they had won the right to be free of taxation by national governments generally. Not only did locals fail to pay the tax, supported publicly by politicians, but groups of vigilantes patrolled the states, tarring and feathering revenue officials and harassing local producers who were known to have paid the tax (Glaser, 1976: 76).

The government retreated slightly, reducing the taxes in 1792 and 1794 (Klein, 1976: 31), but in July 1794 hostilities broke out between a consortium of grain farmers, distillers, shippers, and retailers, and the United States marshal. This was followed by armed assaults on local officials by armed men, resulting in a number of murders. Some seven thousand opponents of the tax mustered in Pittsburgh, and President Washington was forced to send in troops to put down the rebellion. The sight of nearly thirteen thousand soldiers led by the governor of Virginia, General Henry "Light Horse Harry" Lee, and supported by appearances of other generals and even President Washington himself, so frightened the populace that the so-called whiskey rebellion ended without a shot being fired, and the tax was collected forthwith (Glaser, 1976: 75-76, Klein, 1976: 31). The tax was repealed in 1801 by President Thomas Jefferson, but it was reimposed after the Civil War (Klein, 1976: 31).

The whiskey rebellion was important because it was the first large-scale opposition to control of trade in alcohol and also because it established the power of the federal government to impose taxes and controls on alcohol production in the states. There were other whiskey rebellions, although none was as serious as the first. For example, in March 1894, the governor of South Carolina sent the state militia to Darlington to put down a rebellion against the imposition of a state monopoly on alcohol retail and wholesale (the dispensary system). When a significant portion of the troops refused to muster, Governor Tillman was forced to send volunteer "wool hat boys." By April 5 the rebellion had been dispersed, at the cost of three lives (including one man who lingered almost a year before dying of his wounds) (Huggins, 1971: 140-64).

In addition to these open rebellions, there was continual conflict between moonshiners and the revenue and police officials who tried to put them out of business. Moonshining, the production of distilled beverage alcohol at unlicensed, untaxed stills, was an especially prevalent industry in the south starting in the 1880s and continuing until the present day. When whiskey taxes were reimposed after the Civil War, sometimes violent resistance resurfaced. Moonshining increased during economic downturns and was accompanied by vigilante justice, as moonshiners took revenge on informers who led revenue officials to illegal stills, tried to drive rivals out of business, or avenged competitors' attempts to put them out of business (Ayers, 1984: 261-62). Like their ancestors a hundred years earlier, southern whiskey producers in the 1870s believed that the United States was founded for the purpose of being a free republic in which citizens could make their own living without government interference, and they were willing to defend their liberty with violence (Ayers, 1984: 262).

Added to that was the tradition of generations-long blood feuds in the mountains of Kentucky, Virginia, West Virginia, and Tennessee. Conflicts over moonshining, informing, and still-busting sparked many a lengthy conflict, such as the famous feud of the Hatfields and the McCoys. Prohibition only increased the violence as the whole alcohol production industry moved underground, and private vigilantism entirely replaced police regulation of it (Ayers, 1984: 263-64).

Drink and Social Order

By the nineteenth century, the link between alcohol and violence was firmly established in the popular mind. Whereas the colonists drank alcohol with their meals, during the nineteenth century drinking alcohol became detached from mealtimes. Increasingly, taverns were used exclusively for drinking by men, especially immigrant and lower-class men, unlike the colonial establishments that served food and drink to men and women alike. Drinking had become a male activity, taking place away from work and not including the family. It became a time-out behavior, increasingly associated with disinhibition (Parks, 1976: 134-35; Levine, 1983: 127).

These changes in drinking patterns were related to the increasing industrialization of the United States and the rise of a stable middle class. Industrial laborers worked a strict daily and weekly schedule, with special periods set aside for leisure (Levine, 1983: 127). The Friday-night-drunk pattern did not come into being until Friday night was the end of the workweek. And widespread concern with maintaining social order by suppressing inebriation accompanied rising prosperity and an increasing distinction between established Americans and new immigrants, most of whom were from different ethnic or economic groups than the established citizens.

The increasing preoccupation of United States society with social order was reflected in the development of a professional police force and a variety of regulatory agencies (Parks, 1976: 130). Whereas eighteenth-century whiskey producers were outraged by the idea that the federal government wanted to tax and regulate their trade, a hundred years later their descendants turned increasingly to government agencies for legal protection through regulation. The rising middle class was concerned over potential damage to property by drunken carousers and time lost from work by inebriated laborers. They supported expanded police powers and regulation of alcohol.

For example, whereas the state of Massachusetts imposed penalties only for habitual drunkenness before 1835, in that year the law was changed and single instances of drunkenness became punishable. Arrests for drunkenness in Boston numbered in the thousands in the 1840s. The Boston Society for the Suppression of Intoxication made public calls for increased police work to combat drunkenness (Parks, 1976: 135-36).

Boston was especially concerned with the behavior of immigrant Irish. In the same way that opium smoking was only considered a problem when white Californians became concerned over labor competition from Chinese immigrants, alcohol drinking was considered a problem as it was increasingly associated with lower-class and immigrant men (Parks, 1976: 139). At that time ethnic divisions among various European types were deeply felt. Established Americans of English and German descent viewed Irish and Scottish immigrants with the same wary disdain as their European forbears.

The old concept of alcohol as the good creature of God did not die out as temperance ideology, with its emphasis on demon rum proliferated. The twin concepts of good-alcohol and bad-alcohol coexisted. D. Cahalan quotes a local politician in the Mississippi state legislature in 1958 who perfectly captures the dual image of alcohol:

> If, when you say whiskey, you mean the devil's brew, the poison scourge, the bloody monster that defiles innocence, yea, literally takes the bread from the mouths of little children; if you mean the evil drink that topples the Christian man and woman from the pinnacles of righteous, gracious living into the bottomless pit of degradation and despair, shame and helplessness and hopelessness, then certainly I am against it with all of my power.

But if, when you say whiskey you mean the oil of conver-
sation, the philosophic wine, the stuff that is consumed when
good fellows get together, that puts a song in their hearts and
laughter on their lips and the warm glow of contentment in
their eyes; if you mean Christmas cheer; if you mean the stim-
ulating drink that puts spring in the old gentleman's step on a
frosty morning; if you mean the drink that enables a man to
magnify his joy, and his happiness, and to forget, if only for a little while, life's great tragedies and heartbreaks and sorrows, if
you mean that drink, the sale of which pours into our treasuries
untold millions of dollars which are used to provide tender care
for our little children, our blind, our deaf, our dumb, our pitiful
aged and infirm, to build highways, hospitals, and schools, then
certainly I am in favor of it. (Cahalan, 1987: 23-24)

The temperance movement, arising in the middle class in the
early nineteenth century, tried to turn public opinion toward the
bad-alcohol side of the equation. Temperance speakers believed that
social problems such as crime, violence, poverty, and domestic violence were caused by alcohol (Levine, 1983: 129). They promulgated
the idea that even small amounts of liquor would release the inner
beast in any man, leading to violent, dissolute behavior. As John
Marsh wrote in the 1830s, alcohol "makes every man that drinks it
a villain" (cited in Levine, 1983: 133).

Temperance movement members not only promulgated the
disinhibition thesis of the effects of alcohol, they also believed it to
be a dangerously addicting drug that could lead to the total destruction of the drinker's ability to act in a moral fashion. So strong was
their belief in the destructive powers of drink that they thought that
habitual drinkers were permanently morally incapacitated, whether
drunk at the moment or not (Levine, 1983: 135). Temperance writers
claimed that most crime was caused by alcohol:

It is admitted that three-fourths of all the crimes of the land
result from the use of intoxicating liquor. It is admitted that at
least three-fourths of all the sufferings of poverty arise from
the same source. (cited in Levine, 1983: 137)

Temperance ideology was based on the idea that human
beings have a violent, bestial inner nature that is held in check by

social controls and released by disinhibiting drugs such as alcohol. Temperance utilized the concept of moral order, which arose with increasing capitalization and the rise of the concept of society as redeemed by increasingly rational social arrangements. Unlike early settlers who thought social order was maintained by the external pressure of church, family, and community on the individual, nineteenth-century temperance activists thought that social order depended on the personal psychological self-control of individuals, guided by the wisely designed laws of the state (Levine, 1983: 142-44).

With this new concept of the nature of social order and of human nature , alcohol was seen as a dangerous drug and inebriate disinhibition as threatening to the continuing existence of society. In addition, the increasing ethnic and economic diversity of the United States, rather than leading to a melting pot society, produced a series of interrelated but largely segregated subcultures, each viewing the others with fearful suspicion or resentment.

Summary and Implications of Historical Evidence

The historical evidence thus shows that a belief in the notion that alcohol consumption caused violence was well established, especially by the middle of the nineteenth century. This belief was consistent with the historical and contemporary experience of people in the west and the south, the honor system helping to establish this both in the elite classes, with the experience of dueling, and in the working classes, and on the frontier, with the rough and tumble, both being behavior patterns that became closely linked to alcohol consumption and intoxication. All through the late eighteenth and nineteenth centuries, and into the early twentieth century, alcohol consumption was linked to the violence of groups perceived as economic threats to the established groups that had preceded the newer groups to, or were less powerful in, the new world; Native Americans, African-American slaves (and even former slaves after the Civil War), and the more recent immigrant groups like the Irish and the Italians. In each case, alcohol consumption by these groups came to be associated, culturally, with violence.

The association between alcohol and collective violence can be seen as having a legitimating influence on the cultural belief in the link and its empirical manifestations in the eighteenth, nineteenth, and twentieth centuries. To resist any attempt to limit access to alcohol or to tax alcohol production and distribution was transformed into a patriotic fight to resist tyranny. This served to further establish the causal link between alcohol and individual violence, as maintaining ready and inexpensive availability of alcohol was the result of such collective violence associated with alcohol.

The association of alcohol as a cause of violence generally, and not just among those who threatened the stability of dominant groups, was fostered by the growing temperance movements, both before and after the Civil War. This was in some ways a more honest assessment of the facts, because as we have seen, the established groups participated in alcohol-related violence to an extent that was probably as great or greater than those new or 'dangerous' groups did. This was surely influenced by the increasing segregation of drinking as a male activity conducted away from the home and away from family life. This is the beginning of alcohol being associated with the time-out phenomenon described by MacAndrews and Edgerton (1969) with regard to twentieth-century American drinking practices. The increased supply of alcohol that coincided with the increasing industrialization of work, and the separation of work and home that resulted, further exacerbated the problems that alcohol caused, especially violence. These processes, beginning in the early nineteenth century, fed the beginnings of the first wave of temperance in the antebellum period.

A similar phenomenon occurred after the repeal of Prohibition, but this time the cultural basis for the alcohol and violence link was well established. Once the supply of alcohol increased rapidly after 1950 (see figures 4.2 and 5.1), rates of violence and homicide increased, once again giving impetus to a new wave of temperance, overlaid with the idea of alcoholism as a disease and the recovering alcoholic as a disease victim. In sum, then, American culture provides a strong foundation for the link between alcohol and violence. It is the nature of the historical development of that link that explains its existence as uniquely American.

International Comparisons

Given the historical development of the violence and alcohol link described here, just how distinctive do we find the United States to be with regard to homicide rates and alcohol consumption? Table 1.1

gives data on both these variables for twelve major industrialized nations from the Americas, Europe, and Asia. As revealed in table 1.1, the United States far outstrips comparable nations in homicide rates, as well as in consumption of distilled spirits or so-called hard liquor (whiskey, gin, scotch, etc.). Concerning beer consumption, which is currently America's favorite alcoholic beverage (see figure 5.1), the United States ranks about in the middle of the distribution. However, if we take the average homicide rate of the six nations that consume more beer per capita than the United States does, the resulting figure is less than one-fifth of the homicide rate in the United States (8.3 vs. 1.46). Taken together, no other country on this list ranks anywhere near as high on homicide, spirits consumption, and beer consumption as the United States. For example, if we sum the ranks on these three distributions, the United States would score nine; one on homicide, one on spirits, and seven on beer. The next highest joint ranking nation is Canada, with a joint ranking of eleven; two on homicide, one on spirits, and eight on beer consumption. Yet Canada's homicide rate is about one-fourth that of the United States. New Zealand scores fourteen on the combined ranking, again with a homicide rate that is less than one-fourth that of the United States; none of the other nations come close in terms of being simultaneously high on both violence and consumption. Concerning wine, the one alcoholic beverage that the United States lags behind the rest of the industrialized world in consumption of, table 1.1 again shows that the leading wine consumption nations—Italy, France, Austria, Germany—have substantially lower rates of homicide than does the United States. These data reveal the current manifestation of the unique combination of two American traditions, alcohol consumption and homicide.

CHAPTER SUMMARY: THE REST OF THE STORY

The remainder of this book is divided into five chapters. In chapter 2, a detailed set of answers to the questions of how and why alcohol might be related to homicide is discussed. Pre- and metatheoretic assumptions are discussed, and alcohol is put into three major theories from the homicide causation literature: economic deprivation, social bonds/disorganization, and routine activity/lifestyle theory. In each case, the form of the relationship is described, and a set

TABLE 1.1

International Comparisons of Homicide and Alcohol Consumption

Nation	Homicide[1]	Rank	Spirits[2]	Rank	Beer[3]	Rank	Wine[4]	Rank
United States	8.30	1	2.5	1	90	7	9.1	12
Canada	2.10	2	2.5	1	83	8	10.2	11
New Zealand	1.95	3	1.6	8	121	3	15.3	8
Australia	1.90	4	1.2	11	113	5	20.6	5
Italy	1.90	4	1.0	12	26	12	79.0	1
Denmark	1.50	6	1.5	10	125	2	20.4	6
Austria	1.35	7	1.6	8	116	4	32.1	3
Sweden	1.30	8	2.0	6	52	9	11.9	10
France	1.30	8	2.3	3	39	11	75.1	2
West Germany	1.25	10	2.2	5	144	1	25.8	4
Japan	0.90	11	2.3	3	44	10	12.5	9
England/Wales	0.80	12	1.7	7	110	6	17.1	7

[1] Rate per 100,000 population; from National Research Council, 1993: 52
[2] Consumption in liters pure alcohol equivalent per capita; Sparrow et al., 1989
[3] Consumption in liters per adult; Sparrow et al., 1989
[4] Consumption in liters per adult; Sparrow et al., 1989

of testable hypotheses is generated. The second part of chapter 2 compares the results of this theoretical analysis with several recent developments in criminological theory, including control theory (Gottfredson and Hirschi, 1990), structural criminology (Hagan, 1989), and an emotive approach to crime as reflected in Katz's (1988) *Seductions of Crime*. Chapter 3 describes the data bases and discusses the methodological and statistical approaches used in the two analyses reported here.

Chapters 4 and 5 are the two analyses chapters. In chapter 4, a longitudinal structural model of homicide and alcohol availability, which has been found to be sufficiently linked to consumption to be a useful proxy for alcohol consumption (Gruenewald et al., 1993), is presented for United States cities between 1960 and 1980. The results of this analysis show the underlying relationship between alcohol and homicide, and set the stage for the policy based analysis presented in chapter 5. During the 1980s, the United States engaged in a major alcohol control effort directed at reducing alcohol-related problems, especially drunk driving, among youth. This was achieved by forcing states to raise the minimum drinking age from 18 (in most states) to 21. Although this effort has been evaluated in terms of drunk driving and other alcohol-related outcomes (O'Malley and Wagenaar, 1991), no one has considered whether or not this policy change had an impact on youth homicide. The results of chapter 5 reveal that it did, at least in certain types of youth homicide, a finding that will make sense in the context of the theoretical and empirical material presented in the preceding chapters. Finally, chapter 6 presents a summary, some conclusions about what has been learned from this study, some unanswered questions about alcohol and violence, and a preview of work in progress that may address some of these unanswered questions.

Chapter 2

HOW AND WHY SHOULD ALCOHOL
AND HOMICIDE BE RELATED?

In chapter 1 the origins of the link between alcohol and homicide have been described, and sufficient evidence has been provided for the claim that this connection is uniquely American. However, the lack of attention in the field of criminology to this connection has resulted in a theoretical vacuum such that no comprehensive description of how and why alcohol and homicide are related is available. Yet there is not lack of theory in criminology, indeed, this discipline has experienced a theoretical renaissance in the last decade, with the publication of a number of major theoretical works, including but not limited to those by Gottfredson and Hirschi (1990), Hagan (1989), and Katz (1988). In addition, three decades of research on homicide and violence has produced a number of middle-range theories that have made significant contributions to the knowledge base on the causes of homicide. What is clearly needed, then, are theoretical analyses that link alcohol to the substantial body of general and middle-range theories of violence. Initial efforts have been made in this direction by a number of researchers (Fagan, 1990;

Pernanen, 1991; Lenke, 1990; Parker, 1989, 1993a). The theoretical analyses presented here have benefited from these efforts. The task here will be to go beyond those efforts, to make the discussion both more precise by further specification, and broader by describing the linkages between the theoretical models described here and some of the recent major theoretical contributions to criminology.

At least one school of thought, often associated with policy research on topics like alcohol and violence, is much less concerned with theoretical analysis than the approach taken here. If there is a reasonably good chance that alcohol and violence are causally related, so such reasoning goes, why worry about the details, the how and why of the relationship? Cook and Moore (1993a), arguing in this vein, suggest that successful interventions designed to break the alcohol-violence link need not wait upon the discovery of complete understanding of how and why alcohol helps to cause more violence; all that is required is that policies designed to lower rates of alcohol consumption be implemented, and it follows that alcohol-related violence will decline. Although I am sympathetic to this point of view, its application to the alcohol-violence link is misguided for a number of important reasons.

First, so little is known about this relationship and, indeed, with some analysts even suggesting that this relationship is partly or wholly spurious (Collins, 1989), the risk of committing to a policy program that in fact will have no impact on violence is an important one to consider. A number of questions are begged by this "black box" approach, as I will call it here. The most important is why alcohol is related to violence in some situations and not others, which appear, in most details, to be similar to those in which alcohol seems to lead to violence? Another set of questions concern the type of alcoholic beverage and the types of drinking situations that might lead to violence. Without a better understanding of the circumstances under which alcohol and violence are linked, policy implementation risks doing more harm than good, and could, depending on the type of implementation, inadvertently exacerbate alcohol-related violence. A third set of issues involves the inability, under the black box model, to understand how changes in alcohol consumption would affect violence, and therefore have an impact on policies implemented to reduce alcohol-related violence. Since 1980 alcohol consumption in the United States has declined overall, although consumption of specific beverage types has shown divergent trends during this period (Treno, Parker, and Holder, 1993; Treno and Parker, 1993). Unless our understanding of how and why alcohol is related to violence is clear, any change in alcohol consumption that is not monolithic and unidirectional will leave us in the dark as to how our policy intervention will be affected by such changes. Therefore no one can describe the changes in policy that would be needed to accommodate the changing consumption and violence relationship.

Another case for theoretical analysis has been described eloquently by Jasso (1990), and it involves the discovery of new connections and hypotheses that often emerge only once the logic of theoretical analysis is applied to a problem. It is quite clear that a theory involving only alcohol and murder as concepts would be untenable, for the obvious reason that both alcohol and homicide are imbedded in complex social and cultural situations. Unless an attempt is made to analyze the way in which alcohol as one possible causal agent in a model of violence relates to other theoretically important causal agents—for example, poverty, routine activities, social disorganization, and so on—no new hypotheses, reflecting relationships that are unanticipated by conventional approaches, can be derived. It may in fact be this process of theoretical discovery, as Jasso (1990) calls it, which could lead to the most appropriate policy intervention. The "black box" approach could never result in such discovery, and for this reason alone can be rejected in favor of the approach being advocated here.

A MACROSOCIAL APPROACH
TO AN INDIVIDUAL PHENOMENON

Most people think of homicide as an event that involves individuals, at least two individuals, and that to understand homicide one must understand why individuals would get excited enough, angry enough, frustrated enough to kill other individuals. Almost everyone has had such feelings at one time or another, and when they imagine what a murderer and a murderer's victim experience, they tend to think in these individualistic terms. In other cases, people imagine that someone who commits a murder must be insane, suffering from severe mental illness, a belief that is confirmed when well-publicized murder cases end with the accused being declared insane and sentenced to a facility for the criminally insane instead of to prison or to be executed. Although it is the case that homicide has always been part of human society, anyone who examines the way rates of homicide vary across time and space (see table 1.1, chapter 1) is confronted with a dilemma, at least from the individualistic approaches to homicide that many people take. Rates of homicide vary quite dramatically across the societies listed in table 1.1, and as shown by Archer and Gartner (1984), they vary even more dramatically when the list of societies considered is enlarged to include anything close to a majority of extant societies on the globe. If individual characteristics and traits caused homicide, it would have to be the case that the distribution of the characteristics and traits that cause homicide would be differentially distributed in the populations of different nations.

First, with regard to biological traits, there is little or no evidence to suggest that the gene pool differs to any great extent across the nations listed in table 1.1. Indeed, there has been a great deal of migration out of and into most of these nations over the last three hundred years. Japan has not received very many migrants, but other places have received Japanese migrants, so that any genetically distinct traits from the Japanese gene pool have been introduced into the gene pools of several of the other nations in table 1.1. If the term *individual* is meant to refer to characteristics such as personality and temperament, which may be culturally determined, it must be assumed that personality types are distributed differentially in the populations of the societies that have different rates of homicide. There may indeed be culturally determined differences in personality, but even so, research in social psychology suggests that personalities are not as stable as is often assumed across an individual's lifetime (House, 1981). Although a person's culture would not have changed, their personality might, suggesting that culturally determined differences in personality are not stable enough to explain societal-level differences in rates of homicide. Further, research on the connection between personality, attitude, and behavior suggests that situational factors are much more important that personalities and attitudes in predicting behavior (see House, 1981, for a review of social structure and personality research).

If the distribution of individual traits and characteristics does not differ between nations, then this factor is logically unable to account for the differences in rates of violence. This suggests that social structural differences should be considered as viable candidates for explaining the differences in homicide rates. The introduction of alcohol into models of homicide causation presents no problem for this approach, as a similar logic applies: drinking alcoholic beverages is something individuals do, but the circumstances in which people drink alcohol and the amounts individuals consume are most significantly influenced by social structural conditions, as evidenced in a large body of research in the alcohol studies area (Smart, 1977; Cook and Tauchen, 1982; Treno, Parker, and Holder, 1993). Indeed, structural factors have fared well in the research literature on homicide, so that rates of poverty and certain kinds of family structures have been the most consistent predictors of homicide (Loftin and Hill, 1974; Parker, 1989; Sampson, 1987). Thus the *appropriate* level at which to analyze homicide rates in general and the link between alcohol and homicide specifically is a macrosocial one, in which variation in homicide rates can be explained as a function of variation in social structural conditions.

The case for a macrolevel approach becomes even more obvious when considering rates of violence within a single society. Even in the United States, albeit a large and diverse society, but one that shares a common culture, languages, customs, laws, and so on, the rate of homicide varies widely across space. Table 2.1 gives the rates of homicide for several large, medium, and small United States cities for 1980; these data are part of the analysis to be presented in chapter 4.

As these data reveal, the variation in homicide rates within the United States is extreme, with a factor of 60 separating the highest rate (Miami, Florida: 63.43 homicides per 100,000 population) from the lowest rate (Cedar Rapids, Iowa: 0.91; that is the lowest rate for any city that actually recorded at least one homicide). Although a number of dimensions along which Miami differs from Cedar Rapids immediately spring to mind, none of these involve individual traits, either biological or personality-based. There are proportionately as many nice people, obnoxious people, mean people, short people, mentally ill people, overweight people in each of these two communities as well as in the other cities listed in table 2.1. However, where Miami, Cedar Rapids, and other places do differ from one another is in terms of the *structural* conditions of life: population composition, rates of poverty and wealth, age structure, school enrollment, household composition, unemployment, and so

TABLE 2.1
Homicide Rate, Selected U.S. Cities, 1980

City	Homicide Rate	Population
Birmingham, AL	30.94	284,413
Tuscaloosa, AL	13.30	75,211
Phoenix, AZ	13.04	789,704
Inglewood, CA	57.30	94,162
Los Angeles, CA	34.04	2,968,528
Sacremento, CA	16.32	275,741
San Jose, CA	9.85	629,400
Denver, CO	20.11	492,686
New Haven, CT	14.27	126,089
Ft.Lauderdale, FL	28.71	153,279
Miami, FL	63.43	346,689
Peoria, IL	10.47	124,160
Hammond, IN	12.81	93,714
Cedar Rapids, IA	.91	110,243
Wichita, KN	11.46	279,838
Dearborn, MI	3.31	90,660
Detroit, MI	45.46	1,203,368
Minneapolis, MN	9.71	370,951
Jackson, MS	20.70	202,895
Las Vegas, NV	55.87	164,674
Albuquerque, NM	15.07	332,920
New York, NY	25.62	7,071,639
Fayetteville, NC	35.29	59,507
Cleveland, OH	46.18	513,822
Columbus, OH	15.40	565,032
Beaumont, TX	14.40	118,102
Houston, TX	39.68	1,595,138
Seattle, WA	12.76	493,486
Milwaukee, WI	11.63	636,297

on. As it is along these dimensions, as well as on alcohol availability and consumption (as will be discussed in chapter 3), that these places vary, it must be from among these characteristics of places that the explanation for the variation in homicide rates be sought.

On the other hand, because homicide and alcohol manifest themselves in individuals, some assumptions about how this process happens are required if any macrolevel theorizing is to be legitimate. In this fashion micro and macro theorizing can be combined without the risk of improper inferences. Homicide and alcohol consumption are members of a class of phenomena in which the relationship between the individual behavior and the macro manifestation is relatively direct. Individual behavior of this sort adds up to a pattern at the macrolevel, allowing for macrolevel assessments of the implications of individual behavior and interaction. If we can at least propose an explanation of the connection between alcohol and homicide at the individual level, the macrolevel relationship between alcohol consumption and availability and homicide rates can be used to evaluate the likelihood that the individual link proposed may be valid. Obviously, if the macrolevel relationship implied by the microlevel explanation is not found empirically, doubt is cast on the validity of the micro link; if the macro relationship is observed, the case for the micro link is strengthened, and the implications for policies designed to reduce the strength of the individual link are made clearer.

This approach is neither unique nor new to either alcohol research or to the study of homicide. Studies of the link between the average price of alcohol and aggregate consumption are macrolevel studies based on a microlevel relationship that is presumed, not tested, and such studies form the basis of economic policies directed toward the control of alcohol consumption (Cook and Tauchen, 1982; Ornstein and Hanssens, 1985). A large body of research spanning a number of substantive areas is based on Blau's (1977) structural theory, the basis of which is the relative proportion of categories of individuals in a population, and the implications this has for intergroup and intragroup interaction (South and Messner, 1986; Skvoretz, 1983). Although individual homicide events have been the focus of a number of important studies (Luckenbill, 1977; Felson and Steadman, 1983), the most important research on homicide has also taken this micro to macro form (Loftin and Hill, 1974; Land et al., 1990). The major themes in homicide research during the past three decades, involving the impact of poverty, racial composition, and region, are all formulated on the basis of the postulation of an individual effect, which is then reflected in the macrolevel relationship between the homicide rate on the one hand and the poverty rate (Parker, 1989), the proportion of the population that is African-American (Rogers, 1992), and the proportion of the population that is southern (Land et al., 1990).

For a number of important reasons, then, it is important to examine the alcohol and homicide relationship at the macrolevel.

However, before theorizing in detail about the relationships we expect to observe in the aggregate, a discussion of the nature of the alcohol and homicide relationship at the individual level is required.

Selective Disinhibition: A Social Theory of Alcohol and Violence

According to the arguments made thus far, we need to have at the very least a set of plausible assumptions that outline the connection between alcohol and homicide at the individual level in order to proceed with theoretical and empirical research on the connection between rates of consumption/availability and homicide rates at the macrolevel. Once again anyone attempting to establish such a set of plausible assumptions is faced with a dilemma. If detailed accounts of individual homicides are examined (Luckenbill, 1977; Felson and Steadman, 1983; Wilbanks, 1984), it is clear that the social interactions portrayed, until the lethal violence begins, are representative of a very large number social interactions that *do not* end in violence or homicide. So the question that must be addressed is why do *some* situations in which people are engaging in ordinary social interaction, and in which one or more parties to the interaction have been drinking alcohol, end in homicide?

Use of the word *some* in the previous sentence may be misleading, because in fact homicide, despite the relatively high rates in the United States (see table 1.1 and 2.1), is an extremely rare occurrence. Even if we consider all serious assaults as potential homicides (this idea is advanced by some violence researchers, but is by no means universally accepted; see Zimring, 1972; Skogan, 1978), the national rate for the United States from 1990, 424.1 per 100,000 (Federal Bureau of Investigation, 1992), still represents a relatively rare event, especially if one considers that the true denominator for the potential homicide rate could be viewed as almost all interactions between individuals—a huge number, even if certain interactions are eliminated (although a thorough consideration of the details of homicide incidents quickly convinces the skeptic that almost all interactions and relationships between people have the potential for lethal violence). Here we have focused attention on alcohol-involved interactions, but given the degree to which alcohol is an integral part of the lives of most Americans, we are still left with a very large number of potentially dangerous interactions, of which only a very few end in homicide. So whatever role alcohol plays in homicide, it must be dependent on other characteristics of the people and the interactional context in which alcohol and homicide occur. As suggested previously, there is no reason to believe that the distribution of individuals can explain the variations in space that are observed in homicide rates. We are left with the conclusion that some aspect of the social context in which alcohol is consumed and homicide sometimes happens, distinguishes or selects a relatively few of these social situations for the outcome of homicide.

The disinhibition hypothesis has had a checkered history in the field of alcohol research (Room and Collins, 1983, for a thorough review of the issues) and is at this point relatively unfavored by most experts (Pernanen, 1991: 217). However, if disinhibition is linked to the social selection argument outlined here, a more sophisticated and more plausible hypothesis can be constructed, one that is much closer to both ordinary experience and to what is currently known about alcohol and homicide. The way to do this is to argue that there is a socially derived, selectively active disinhibition process, involving norms that condemn interpersonal violence as a viable tool for the resolution of disputes. This is one mechanism whereby the selectivity dilemma identified previously can be addressed, helping therefore to explain why it is that only a very small number of social interactions involving alcohol lead to homicide.

Selective Disinhibition:
The Process and Some Illustrations

How would this social, selective disinhibition work? If we define *constraint* as the impact that norms have on individual behavior—that is, the degree to which an individual does not act contrary to normative expectations—regardless of whether the source of the constraint is internal (Gottfredson and Hirschi, 1990) or external (Akers, 1973), we can define that individual's behavior as constrained. Further, constraint can be divided into two general types, active and passive. Active constraint is defined as constraint in which the circumstances of the social interaction are such that using X behavior (X being equal to any behavior of this type an individual might choose) to address others in the setting is desirable, but contrary to normative expectations. Similarly, passive constraint is when the social situation is such that the use of the normatively contrary behavior is perceived to be against the individual's interests, or contrary to their goals. Another way of describing the active/passive constraint distinction is that in the former case, one is tempted to engage in a certain behavior, but chooses not to do so, whereas in the latter, the nature of the social situation is such that the temptation is diminished or removed entirely.

Selective disinhibition operates through the interplay of passive and active constraint—that is, the way norms affect behavior, and the social setting of that behavior—including alcohol consumption. It is clear that most people, experts and nonexperts, believe that alcohol can disinhibit some kinds of constraints in some situations. This is the case, once again, regardless of the source of the disinhibition—expectancies (Leigh, 1989; Christiansen et al., 1985), Timeout behavior (McAndrews and Edgerton, 1969), or something else entirely. In the logic of this approach, then, alcohol leads to homicide when the situation is one in which violence is a potentially useful approach, as perceived by at least one actor, and alcohol has been consumed by at least that same actor. Active constraint would be required in this type of interaction on the part of the actor who perceives that violence would be useful; the disinhibiting effect of alcohol is to undermine the operation of active constraint in such a situation. In all likelihood this is a sort of threshold effect, with the location of the threshold also dependent on the particular situation and the individuals involved, so that the same amount of consumption might be sufficient to overcome active constraint in one situation and not sufficient in a similar situation. This effect should be seen as a continuum, along which there is a point when active constraint is overcome and violence results. The reason why, therefore, that relatively few situations involving alcohol lead to violence is that a particular set of conditions needs to be met, and a threshold, which may vary even among the same individuals across similar situations, needs to be reached and surpassed.

It should also be noted that active and passive constraint operate and can be overcome in the absence of alcohol consumption, but that because alcohol can have a disinhibiting effect on behavior, the presence of alcohol tends to enhance the possibility of disinhibition of active constraint, and thus to increase the likelihood of violence (Stets, 1990; Fagan, 1990). Some detailed illustrations are in order at this point so that the operation of the selective disinhibition process can be seen more clearly. Two types of illustrations will be described: first some hypothetical situations will be presented, and then some actual homicide case summaries will be examined with the concepts of selective disinhibition and active/passive constraint in hand.

Hypothetical Illustrations

If we apply the simplifying assumptions that two actors are in isolation from others in these situations, the way in which this process might work can be described as follows. Two individuals are having a dispute about the possession of some object each considers to have some value. The value of the object may be substantial or insubstantial; all that is assumed is that both actors desire the object and are not inclined to yield to the demand of the other for possession of the object. Assuming that the actors are normal adults, in the broadest sense of both those descriptors, one or both of these actors may perceive that violence would be a useful strategy in settling the dispute over possession of the object. In nonalcohol-involved situations, violence is an unlikely outcome, although the probability of violence in any such dispute is not zero. Active constraint is likely to be operating in the case of both actors; although one or both may have the thought that violence could lead to possession of the object, norms that require individuals in everyday interaction to refrain from engaging in violence in such disputes are upheld.

Suppose that we retain the circumstances of this first example, except that we endow one actor with a substantial advantage in power. This could derive from a number of sources: social, economic, political, physical. However, the impact of active constraint in this modified situation would be largely restricted to the power-advantaged actor. Enhanced by this advantage, violence would be an even more effective (although less necessary) means of obtaining possession of the object. However, the power-deprived actor would be subject to passive constraint; because of the fact that violence is no longer a viable option, this actor would be much less inclined to engage in such behavior, even in the presence of something that might disinhibit violent behavior.

If we now introduce alcohol consumption into these situations, with another simplifying assumption that both parties have had a sufficient amount of alcohol to place them equally under the influence, in the first case the likelihood of violence is significantly increased. Since both actors, with relatively equal power of whatever sort in the situation, are subject to active constraint, the disinhibiting effect of the alcohol consumption may lead one or both to reach and pass the point at which violence is an effective, but not utilized, strategy. Note that even though the likelihood of violence is significantly increased, it still may be relatively rare, as we begin with the fact that violence in interaction is extremely rare, given the population of interactions.

In the second example, the impact of alcohol would also be to enhance the likelihood of violence, although to a lesser degree than in the first example. The power-advantaged actor may disinhibit active constraint under the influence of alcohol because of a perception that such a strategy would not only be effective, but perhaps a quicker and easier solution to the dispute than the use of other kinds of social power this actor may possess. Power of different sorts can have a number of constraints on usage, and therefore violence may be the simpler of alternatives. The power disadvantaged actor is less likely to be disinhibited in this case, since passive constraint, rather than active constraint, is operating on this actor. However, as research on power and power usage has shown, even the most disadvantaged actor will sometimes resort to power usage under certain circumstances (Cook and Emerson, 1978; Cook et al., 1987), so that this actor might also decide that violence is an effective strategy. However, because violence is perceived by this actor to be less likely to succeed than other strategies, even under the influence of alcohol violence is less likely for the power-disadvantaged actor.

A number of comments are in order concerning these illustrations. First, these examples are described as if the actors involved, even under the influence of alcohol, are rational actors, by which we take to mean that they are actors who have consciously made behavioral choices that are directed toward some goal and that the actors perceive will enhance their chances of achieving this goal. This may seem an unlikely set of assumptions for actors that may be under the influence of alcohol. It is well known that alcohol has negative effects on judgment, information processing, and perception (Taylor and Leonard, 1983; Pihl et al., 1993), and it may do so by disorganizing prefrontal brain activity (Pihl et al., 1993). However, taking all these effects as given, people under the influence of alcohol appear,

within limits imposed by the effect of alcohol on judgment, information processing, perception, and the like, to have goals in mind
and to attempt behaviors that, rightly or wrongly from the point of
view of others, they believe will help them achieve those goals
(Pernanen, 1991).

In addition, a key feature of these hypothetical examples is the
way in which alcohol interacts with social factors in the situation.
Many social scientists ultimately rejected the disinhibition hypothesis as originally proposed in alcohol research because it presumed
that alcohol had similar effects—that is, biochemical effects—on
individuals, so that disinhibition ought to operate with reasonable
consistency across social situations. Cross-cultural evidence dis-
pelled this notion of consistency of the effect of alcohol, thus casting
doubt on the entire disinhibition approach. However, the introduction of a mechanism, operating through the interplay of active and
passive constraint and the nature of the situation, shows how disinhibition can operate in some cases and not in others, thus addressing
a major flaw in the original disinhibition approach. This mechanism
can also explain why the vast majority of alcohol-involved situations do not result in violence.

Selective Disinhibition Applied to
Homicide Case Summaries

William Wilbanks published a very enlightening book in 1984 enti-
tled *Murder in Miami*. Among other things this monograph repro-
duces case narratives for every homicide that occurred in 1980 in
Dade County. These narratives were written by Wilbanks, based on
examinations of the files of the medical examiner, the police department, and on interviews with homicide detectives (Wilbanks, 1984:
5). The nature of the arguments that buttress the selective disinhibition hypothesis may become clearer and more concrete if we apply
them to some actual cases of homicide. Please note that the interpretation of these cases of homicide in light of the theoretical arguments made here is completely independent of the arguments presented by Wilbanks (1984), and in no way should be taken as
representing his conclusions.

The first case involves a bar fight in which one man assaulted
the female companion of the other (all three individuals had been
drinking together at the bar). The other man then struck the first

man, according to testimony, in retaliation for the assault on his female companion (Wilbanks, 1984: 195, case #028). This would seem to be a situation in which the type of action engaged in by the first man (who was eventually killed as a result of the bar fight) might have been a less violent interaction with the female companion of his fellow drinker if not for the influence of alcohol. Similarly, if active constraint on the part of the victim had not broken down, it seems unlikely that the offender in this case would have reacted with violence. It is possible, of course, that this same set of interactions could have occurred without the presence of alcohol, but it is reasonable to assume that alcohol's impact was to increase the likelihood that violence would occur.

The second case selected here is also one in which it seems likely that alcohol had some influence on the nature of the interaction. A man and a women are interacting in a pool hall, and during a dispute the male flings two pool balls at the female and hits her, causing a serious enough injury that she was taken to the hospital by the owner of the establishment (1984: 241, case #009). The pool ball flinger, having been evicted by the management, returned and was killed by one of the staff while trying to forcibly reenter the pool hall. Once again, the fact that the pool ball flinger had been drinking (the autopsy revealed a blood alcohol level of .15) was important in the choice of behavior, pool ball flinging, with which this person attempted to solve his dispute with the woman in the pool hall. This act was reasonably effective, in the sense that the dispute with his fellow pool player was settled, although it led to an additional dispute with the management of the pool hall. The fact that he returned with gun, ready to use additional violence to settle this additional dispute, is a further example of active constraint being overcome by the presence of alcohol.

The third example illustrates how, in direct disputes between two people who have been known to be drinking, active constraint is overcome for both people, so that the outcome with regard to who is the victim and who is the offender depends more on chance and the availability of superior weapons (Lauretsen, et al., 1991). This case (Wilbanks, 1984: 245, case #041) involves two individuals who had been drinking and gambling together. The dispute involved a gambling debt, and as the dispute became more heated, one individual shoved the other; he shoved this person again, and the latter pulled out a gun and shot the person who shoved him. So both victim and offender were able to overcome the constraints against violence to settle their dispute. Although as before, this case could have happened as it did without alcohol, alcohol probably led to an increased probability that violence would result.

The last example from Wilbanks (1984: 305, case #519) illustrates the point made previously about actors with different levels of power in the situation and the impact of alcohol on active constraint. In this case a heterosexual couple were drinking together and got into a dispute; the female accused the male of having an affair with another woman. The male may have had a number of options in this case, but decided to stab his companion, and the inference we can make is that the presence of alcohol led to the breakdown of active constraint sufficient enough for the offender to engage in extreme violence.

One fact that should be noted here is that these cases are drawn from Anglo, African American, and Latino groups, so that considering all the 559 homicides in Dade County in 1980, the distribution of alcohol involvement as well as other characteristics differs little if at all across population subgroups. This is further evidence for the notion that structural, rather than individual, characteristics must be considered at the root of homicide variation.

In addition, these cases illustrate that although most people normally think of alcohol as influencing the offender to engage in violent behavior, real homicide interactions are much more complex than the heuristic models often used in social research. Even if alcohol is only present in the blood stream of one party in the dispute, and that individual is seen as the victim in the end, it can be the case that alcohol played a causal role through the disinhibition of active constraint in the ultimate victim. A case reported in Wilbanks (1984: 253, Case #118), in which an individual went to the residence of a drug dealer under the guise of being a customer, but with a plan to rob the dealer, illustrates this point. The victim, who had every intent of being the offender, was more than legally intoxicated at the time of the homicide (autopsy revealed a blood alcohol level of .14, even though the body was found the morning after the event). It is possible that the dealer who shot the victim had not been drinking at all, but alcohol's role as a causal agent is clear. This case is also very consistent with a number of ethnographic accounts of the behavior of so-called career criminals who invariably use alcohol as a means of preparation in the commission of robberies, assaults, and homicides (Samuels, 1976; for a review of a number of such studies, see Roizen, 1981).

Based on the selective disinhibition hypothesis at the individual level, with the concomitant inference that alcohol makes violence more likely in interpersonal disputes via this mechanism, we can make the macrolevel inference that higher rates of alcohol consumption would be associated with higher levels of homicide. However, the manner in which higher alcohol consumption is associated with higher homicide at the macrolevel could take a number of forms. If one or two forms are more likely than the others, our ability to empirically test the alcohol and homicide link, and by implication the apparent validity of the underlying assumptions of selective disinhibition, depends on the a priori enumeration of the different forms, to which we turn next.

Forms of the Alcohol and Homicide Relationship

The very best theoretical discussion of the forms that the alcohol and violence link might take was presented by Pernanen (1981), and the discussion here deals with a subset of his enumeration, which contains the most relevant forms for the purpose at hand. Perhaps the most obvious form this relationship might take is for alcohol to have a direct, independent relationship with homicide. Although most analysts reject such a simplistic view (Collins, 1981; Pernanen, 1981; Fagan, 1990), it is also noted in these sources that there is very little direct evidence from research on homicide in which alcohol consumption is measured and included in the analysis along with other important predictors of homicide. Furthermore, in two recent studies that have included explicit measures of alcohol consumption along with other predictors of violence, consumption had an independent effect on family violence in one case (Stets, 1990) and on homicide in the other (Parker, 1992b). Although the discussion of selective disinhibition presented here also implies that alcohol consumption's relationship with homicide is more complex than this form suggests, because of the macrolevel analyses to be presented here, the direct, net effect of alcohol consumption or availability is one way in which macrolevel results would be consistent with the microlevel assumptions upon which this research is based. The fact that other forms of this relationship may also be indicative of the validity of the underlying assumptions involved in selective disinhibition poses no logical problem. Selective disinhibition, if true, addresses some of the difficulties that have arisen in attempts to explain the link between alcohol and homicide, and therefore examining the validity of this approach, however indirectly, is important scientifically and, as will be seen here, within the policy-making arena. Direct effects of alcohol must also be included in any analysis of interaction effects of alcohol and other factors of importance for homicide research, and so for a number of reasons the analyses presented here will always include direct effects of alcohol on homicide.

A second form that the relationship of alcohol to homicide might take is that alcohol could serve as an intervening or mediating factor between homicide and some other factor thought to be an important cause of homicide. One example is the hypothesis, examined by Parker (1992b), that the long-recognized link between the southern region of the United States and high homicide rates could be explained by the intervening variable of alcohol consumption in the south. This region has lower overall rates of alcohol consumption as compared to other parts of the United States, but substantial evidence suggests that this overall figure masked a more complex relationship. This region has many more lifetime abstainers than do other regions, and therefore it is thought that southerners who drink have, in fact, much higher rates of consumption as compared with drinkers in other parts of the United States (Room, 1983; NIAAA, 1985, 1987). If this higher rate of consumption involves relatively high consumption per occasion, with relatively infrequent occasions per time period, the drinking style that this type of consumption pattern represents is the one that has been most often linked to violence (Room, 1972, 1989; Parker, 1993b). One method to test for this process would be to develop a measure of alcohol consumption per drinker (by subtracting an estimate of abstainers from the population used to calculate the rate of consumption) and include this adjusted consumption measure in a model that also includes a regional indicator and homicide rates. If this form of the relationship is correct, the relationship between region and homicide will go to zero once consumption per drinker is entered into the model. In one study in which this approach was taken, the results were not very promising, so that in four of five homicide types examined, the southern regional indicator remained a significant predictor of homicide with adjusted alcohol consumption included in the model (Parker, 1992b). In the fifth case, robbery homicide rates, an earlier study found that the southern regional indicator was not a significant predictor of this type of homicide, and in that case alcohol consumption was not included in the model (Loftin and Parker, 1985).

Another way this form of the alcohol/homicide relationship could be examined involves a more complex multiequation model in which both the determinants of alcohol consumption and homicide are simultaneously modeled. Although this latter approach will not be utilized here, in the context of the interpretation of the results presented in chapter 5, an illustration of how such a model could be specified will be presented, and some ongoing research designed to evaluate such a model will be described. For the purposes of this study, however, the complexity of multiequation models will be avoided in the interests of a basic examination of the alcohol and homicide relationship.

A third form of the alcohol and homicide relationship considered here is that alcohol might interact with other factors that explain homicide, so that alcohol's impact would be to change the relationship observed between these other factors and homicide. This is probably the most interesting possibility, as well as the most likely one to be found empirically, for a number of reasons. An interaction between alcohol and some other variable that predicts homicide is interesting because interaction relationships could help pinpoint the places or situations where intervention might be most effective. For example, if there were an interaction between alcohol and poverty, the latter being a major predictor of homicide (Parker, 1989), so that places with both high rates of consumption and poverty were places with the highest homicide rates, this would suggest that any interventions designed to reduce alcohol-related violence be focused on places with higher rates of poverty and consumption. In fact, evidence was found at the United States state level of an interaction between poverty and consumption (Parker, 1992b), and a similar hypothesis, described in greater detail below, will be tested in the model reported on in chapter 4. Interaction effects seem most probable from an empirical point of view based on the nature of the behavioral assumptions made here—namely, that alcohol sometimes leads to violence. It is likely that the characteristics of the social structure reflect some of the variation in circumstances under which the alcohol/violence connection will be activated. For example, the combination of a younger population and alcohol consumption might be associated with an increase in disputes involving young males in which alcohol is present in one or both actors, and in which the breakdown of active constraint against violence in such disputes is more likely to occur. Indeed, a younger population has been associated with both increased homicide rates (Cohen and Land, 1987) and increased alcohol consumption (Treno, Parker, and Holder, 1993) in the period since 1950. This is one of three interaction hypotheses that will be tested in the analysis presented in chapter 4.

Finally, for the purposes of this discussion, alcohol and homicide could appear to be related only because there is a third factor that causes both consumption and homicide rates to increase. If the poverty example is reconsidered, it might be the case that the frustration that arises from extreme poverty is actually the cause of both higher consumption and higher rates of violence. If this form of the relationship were the most appropriate, any model of homicide in which alcohol and poverty (or whichever third factor was the common cause of consumption and homicide) were both included would show that homicide was not related to consumption once poverty was controlled for. However, the accumulated evidence and individual level assumptions previously discussed suggest that homicide and alcohol are in fact related. In any case, the proof of the spurious nature of the alcohol/homicide relationship is in the empirical pudding, to paraphrase an old saying; the results presented in chapters 4 and 5 will allow us to dispense with this form rather quickly.

Macrolevel Theoretical Models
to be Tested in Chapter 4

The analysis to be presented in chapter 4 of this volume will examine the direct effects of alcohol availability, an indicator of alcohol consumption (Holder and Wagenaar, 1990; Holder, 1989a; Blose and Holder, 1987). It will also include tests of three interaction hypotheses in which the combined effects of alcohol availability and measures derived from the routine activity/lifestyles approach (Hindelang et al., 1978; Cohen and Felson, 1979); social bonds/social control theory (Hirschi, 1969; Thornberry, 1987), and economic deprivation (Loftin and Hill, 1974; Parker, 1989). The theoretical derivation of these three hypotheses will be described here. This chapter will conclude with a discussion of how the theoretical analysis upon which this study rests relates to other recent theories of crime causation.

Routine Activities and Alcohol: Age and Availability

The logic behind the notion that changes in routine activities (Cohen and Felson, 1979) or lifestyles (Hindelang et al., 1978) would have an impact on homicide involves a consideration of the basic notion of risk and the relationship of risk to activities that individuals engage in on a regular or routine basis. The label *lifestyles* is often used in this perspective because it becomes clear upon the most superficial level that the kinds of daily routines and activities that individuals engage in are often clustered around certain lifestyles that members of social categories or groups exhibit. For example, the group referred to by the now familiar term *yuppies* (young, upwardly mobile *professionals*) is descriptive of a constellation of activities and routines involving working long hours, going out at night for entertainment, food, and other services, purchasing certain "upscale" commodities like designer clothes or imported cars, and so on. In general, the observation that age is directly correlated with certain constellations of regular activities—that is, a certain set of related lifestyles—has been a major engine of research on the impact of routine activities and lifestyles on violence (Miethe et al., 1987; Sampson and Wooldredge, 1987) and homicide (Gartner, 1990).

Young people engage in riskier routine activities, such as spending a greater proportion of time away from home, going out at night for food and entertainment. These activities are riskier because of the relationship between targets, motivated offenders, and potential guardians described in this perspective (Cohen et al., 1981). If individuals routinely go out at night, they expose themselves to 1) a larger pool of potential offenders and 2) less effective potential guardianship, as compared with staying at home. If individuals live alone, then the dwelling itself provides some guardianship. If others also live in the household, these individuals both provide guardianship while the person is at home and form a smaller pool of potential offenders than if the individual was away from home. Others in the household can, and often do, make a very effective pool of potential offenders, but it is also the case that family homicide rates—that is, in which both offender and victim are family members—have been relatively stable over the last several decades in the United States, while the rate of nonfamily homicide has increased (Loftin and Parker, 1985; Williams and Flewelling, 1987; Federal Bureau of Investigation, 1992).

Places with younger populations are, according to this per-spective, more likely to exhibit higher homicide rates, a relation-ship that could be enhanced by greater alcohol availability and con-sumption. The routine seeking of food and entertainment outside the home at night could be enhanced by greater availability of places that serve alcohol, and one of the routine activities engaged in could be the purchasing of alcohol at liquor stores. More availability of these types of establishments would mean greater exposure to risk, independent of the impact that alcohol may have on the course of interpersonal disputes, as previously outlined. Therefore, through greater exposure to risk in alcohol acquisition behavior and because of the associated higher levels of consumption and the impact of alcohol itself on homicide, the interaction of availability and a younger average age of the population in a city could lead to higher rates of homicide.

Poverty and Alcohol: Children in
One-Parent Households and Availability

The theoretical and empirical link between poverty and homicide has long been established (Loftin and Hill, 1974). It is one of the most consistent findings in the homicide literature that higher poverty leads to higher rates of homicide (Bailey, 1984; Loftin and Parker, 1985; Sampson, 1987; Land et al., 1990). Poverty may expose individ-uals to more interpersonal disputes over scarce resources, and it also limits the options an individual has available to deal with such dis-putes. Given the relatively cheap price of a least some forms of alcohol in the United States (Treno, Nephew, Ponicki, and Gruenewald, 1993), the effects of alcohol in places with larger proportions of the popula-tion in poverty would be to enhance what has been found to be a strong positive relationship. One recent study has examined the effect of alcohol consumption and poverty on homicide rates at the state level. It found evidence in support of the notion that in places with higher rates of consumption, the relationship between poverty and homicide is substantially stronger than it is in places with average or below-average rates of consumption (Parker, 1993b).

One indicator of poverty that has been used in a number of studies is the proportion of children who live with only one parent (Loftin and Hill, 1974; Parker and Smith, 1979; Smith and Parker, 1980; Messner, 1983a). This measure has also been used as an indicator of the combined effects of social and economic deprivation in order to understand the differences in violent crime rates of African-Americans and Anglo-Americans (Sampson, 1987). The combination of higher availability and higher proportions of children living with one parent should lead to even higher rates of homicide than either measure alone, because alcohol would enhance the link between poverty and homicide.

Social Bonds and Alcohol: Availability and Attachment to Traditional Institutions

Social bonds that tie individuals to each other and to larger social collectives have played a key role in the understanding of how crime and violence come about. One of the most influential statements of this approach is that of Hirschi (1969), in which attachment to traditional institutions like home, school, and the work place help to control the assumed tendency to commit deviant acts on the part of the individual. This control occurs both because the individuals have a relatively important investment in these traditional institutions, by virtue of the time spent in them and the rewards available from these institutions, as well as from the fact that others in these same institutions can exercise a form of social control on an individual's behavior (Krohn, 1991:301-2). The impact of alcohol on this process may be to undermine it, so that social bonds of the type emphasized in this approach would tend to break down in the presence of high rates of alcohol consumption. For example, the type of social control that members of these institutions may be able to exercise probably depends on the effectiveness of active constraint. Although some forms of social control used in families and schools may involve physical violence, the vast majority of interaction in these institutions is nonviolent. However, nonviolent means of control may become ineffective if members of these institutions, under the influence of alcohol, overcome active constraint and use violence in response to attempts at social control.

Alcohol use has normally been seen as a form of deviance to be explained in this approach, and indeed attachment to conventional institutions has been found to be negatively associated with alcohol use among juveniles (Krohn and Massey, 1980). However, the basic form of this relationship may be one in which higher alcohol consumption reduces the effectiveness of attachment to institutions, thus leading to higher rates of homicide. The combination of low levels of social bonds and high rates of consumption would have the strongest relationship with homicide in this form of the relationship.

One way to examine this interactional hypothesis is to combine alcohol availability with an indicator of below-average levels of social bonds, as measured by school enrollment, percent employed, and the proportion of people who live in households with others (that is, the proportion that do not live alone). Such a measure would tap the situation in which alcohol availability combines with low levels of attachment to institutions and should reflect the undermining of bonds by alcohol consumption implied by this line of reasoning. This interaction term would be positively associated with homicide, net of the main effects of social bonds and availability.

Recent Developments in Theoretical Criminology and the Importance of Alcohol

Criminology has recently benefited from a theoretical expansion, of which the arguments presented here about alcohol's role in homicide through active constraint, and the interaction of alcohol with other causes of homicide, is just one example (Fagan, 1990; Stets, 1990; Parker, 1993a). Although there have been a number of recently published theoretical statements or summaries of theoretical approaches that have been developed, the three that seem both the most important and influential, and at the same time most directly related to the theoretical approach described here are Katz's *Seductions of Crime* (1988), Hagan's *Structural Criminology* (1989), and Gottfredson and Hirschi's *A General Theory of Crime* (1990). Each will be discussed in turn, and the link(s) between the main thrust of the arguments contained in these works and the line of reasoning followed here will be described. This will help to place the current work in the context of the larger field of criminology and encourage the sort of integration in theoretical analysis that the field is in need of and of which the current work is an example.

Emotions of Crime and the Influence of Alcohol

Social science and particularly sociology has recently come to recognize the contribution to behavior and the distinctiveness of emotions as a realm for research and theoretical analysis. *Seductions of Crime* (Katz, 1988) is a major contribution to the effort to remind criminologists and others who study violence that the emotive side of this kind of behavior has been neglected for too long and is, in fact, an important aspect of the way violent behavior occurs, why it occurs, and of the recent increases in violence that concern scientist and citizen alike. Most theories of violence have focused, whether explicitly or implicitly, on the rational or goal-directed aspects of violent behavior. This includes, in a very explicit way, the discussion presented here of how alcohol consumption is related to the risk of homicide in interpersonal disputes. However, in another sense the approach detailed here is an attempt to explain how, under some circumstances, everyday rules of conduct that explicitly prohibit violence, in part because of a rational assessment of the consequences that such violation of norms would entail, break down because of the influence of alcohol.

The selective disinhibition approach outlined here helps explain, in Katz's terms, how humiliation is transformed into rage (1988: 22-31). Katz (1988: 21) acknowledges the role of alcohol, but does not discuss the impact of alcohol on the process whereby individuals who are humiliated by those they consider to be their closest associates, friends, and loved ones can turn this humiliation into rage and revenge through violence. As it is the most completely rational response that is represented by active constraint—that is, "you should not use violence in this situation, even if it is to your advantage"—we can perhaps understand the term *advantage* in terms of the emotional response to the situation in which it becomes obvious that violence is an effective alternative. Alcohol, with its well-demonstrated effects on informational intake and processing (Taylor and Leonard, 1983; Pihl et al., 1993), may help the offender to value the emotional satisfaction that comes from an immediate and final solution to the dispute through homicide. Katz refers to this as "righteous slaughter" (1988:12), and in many cases he describes, it seems likely that the offender who experiences an emotional justification or satisfaction at the time of the killing had been drinking.

In short, the process described here as selective disinhibition may in fact have a significant emotional component that alcohol helps to create and enhance in certain situations. The fact that alcohol is so often present in the highly emotionally charged crime of passion situation, described by Katz and others (Wolfgang, 1958; Luckenbill, 1977) suggests that alcohol plays a part in the emotive aspects of violence that Katz has redirected attention to. On the other hand, selective disinhibition also allows for some form of rationality to be recognized in these situations by emphasizing the notion that active constraint must be overcome for violence and homicide to result. The emotive aspect of the situation that Katz discusses could still be important but homicide would not result. Perhaps it is the combination of short term effectiveness of violence in some cases and the emotional satisfaction achieved by such violence that may lead to a more comprehensive analysis of homicide. This work is focused on the former, although the combination of the emotions of violence and the rationality of violence may be an important direction for further investigation.

Structural Criminology and Alcohol: Power, Class Relations, and Structural Outcomes

Hagan's *Structural Criminology* (1989) is a collection of works by Hagan and various associates that provides a number of examples of the application of a theoretical approach that is not so new in terms of its basic principles but rather in the conceptualization of the structural causes of crime. As Hagan (1989: 2-3) points out, a number of important theoretical approaches in criminology have focused attention on the impact of larger structural forces on crime and the application of sanctions to individuals thought to be criminals. However, previous approaches have failed to recognize the primary impact of structure on individuals, that being the class-based, relational aspects of power. As the dominant source of power for the vast majority of people in industrialized societies is related to paid employment, Hagan argues that the most crucial aspect of any structural approach to criminology is to account for the influence of the relative positions of individuals and other actors vis-à-vis the social organization of work (1989:4). Hagan illustrates this point with discussions of three areas of research—white-collar crime, sentencing, and the role of family in delinquency—and in each case he shows how the standard approaches used in these areas suffer from their lack of attention to class-based relational power, whether applied to the causes of corporate or organization homicide, the impact of race on sentencing outcomes, or the relationship of parental employment and gender differences in delinquency (1989: 3-14).

Hagan's discussion of corporate homicide is interesting in the context of this research on the link between alcohol and violence in that the idea that corporate actors are responsible for a form of violence is not often recognized, both in research and in society. This argument recognizes the role of corporate resources and power on outcomes that go far beyond strictly economic concerns, and it is here that Hagan's structural approach can be linked with the current research. The concentration of social and economic power in the hands of a relatively few corporations and individuals has a variety of outcomes that have serious consequences, like violence and death, for those who are powerless as individuals and as members of groups who are excluded from power.

In the aftermath of the Los Angeles riot of April 1992, one of the more controversial issues involved the fact the south central section of the city had what seemed to many an overabundance of liquor stores (*Los Angeles Times*, 7/27/92); it is the case in almost every city of any size in the United States that there are sections in which alcohol outlets are highly concentrated. A strictly economic analysis may not be able to explain such concentrations, for it is the case that in general higher income leads to more consumption (Treno, Newphew, Ponicki, and Gruenewald, 1993). Thus it would seem economically more appropriate to distribute liquor outlets more evenly, or even to concentrate them in middle- and upper-income areas of cities. However, certainly since the 1920s and perhaps even before that, locations with alcohol outlets have been seen as undesirable. The state of California, for example, once had a statute that prohibited liquor stores and bars within a one-mile radius of a college campus. It seems likely that the higher rates of outlet concentration are another outcome of the relative power of alcohol producers and wholesalers who supply liquor outlets, banks that lend money to store owners, and state regulators whose activities may be more oriented toward the interests of alcohol-industry lobbying groups than the regulation of that industry, and the relative powerlessness of the poor and unemployed individuals and groups who live in greater concentration in these areas of high-outlet density. The close connection between availability of alcohol outlets and consumption, as well as the increased rates of homicide that have been predicted here on the basis of greater availability, could be interpreted as an aspect of class-based, relational power differences in Hagan's framework. Any attempt to reduce the impact of alcohol on violence will have to deal successfully with the structural power relations surrounding the alcohol industry if it is to have a chance of actually reducing alcohol-related violence.

A General Theory of Crime and Alcohol: Self-Control and Active Constraint

The publication of Gottfredson and Hirschi's *A General Theory of Crime* (1990) is another example of the major contribution of Travis Hirschi to the study and understanding of crime and its causes. The connection between Hirschi's social-bond approach and the impact of alcohol on violence has already been described, and constitutes one of three major interaction hypotheses examined in chapter 4. In a sense the general theory of crime, which emphasizes the role of self-control as a cause of crime, is a reasonable extension of the idea that social bonds are part of the explanation of why some people commit crime like homicide while most people in society do not. Some critics of the earlier approach have suggested that social-bonds theory offers no mechanism for how attachment to conventional institutions explains criminality (Krohn, 1991), but self-control, developed through socialization (Gottfredson and Hirschi, 1990: 96), which takes place in those very institutions, provides such a mechanism. Thus, self-control prevents people from committing crimes because it requires people to consider long-term consequences (over the short-term gains of crime), to value gains earned from diligence and persistence (over more easily obtained immediate gains), to consider the risk to themselves in the commission of a criminal act (over the excitement that such an act generates), and to consider the pain and suffering of victims of their act as important (versus valuing their own concerns first and foremost) (Gottfredson and Hirschi, 1990: 89).

In terms of the concept of active constraint discussed here, it requires self-control to keep active constraint from being overwhelmed, and violence being used to solve an interpersonal dispute in the situation in which violence provides an advantageous solution to the immediate problem. On the other hand, in the situation of passive constraint, in which violence would provide no gain or excitement, and be unlikely to result in the injury of others, even individuals with relatively low self-control would be less likely to engage in violence. In this sense the common situations in which violence can occasionally occur provide a window through which the concepts of self-control and constraint are complementary and useful for a theoretical understanding of the causes of violence.

Gottfredson and Hirschi explicitly deal with alcohol on several occasions, and in the main they argue that alcohol use and criminality are both the result of a lack of self-control (1990:140). If much of what has been discussed so far in this analysis is to be considered reasonable, this may be somewhat off the mark with regard to alcohol. Perhaps for juveniles, for which the use of alcohol is treated as delinquent, a case could be made, but even there socially but not legally approved alcohol use by juveniles is well integrated into social and cultural life in the United States. Gottfredson and Hirschi (1990: 41, 179) are closer to the implications of the current analysis when they suggest that alcohol might serve to disinhibit certain kinds of responses to the behavior of others or to increase the likelihood that someone will focus on short-term rather than long-term goals or consequences. This line of reasoning is very similar to that discussed previously in this chapter and very consistent with the process of selective disinhibition detailed here. In a sense the present approach may be considered to be conceptually correlative to that taken by Gottfredson and Hirschi, albeit with a much more specific focus on violence and the role of alcohol as a cause of violence.

SUMMARY

The main purpose of this chapter has been to describe in some detail the theoretical and conceptual underpinnings of the selective disinhibition approach to understanding how and why alcohol has a causal influence on homicide. In addition, three major hypotheses, in which alcohol is seen as combining with concepts of other theories of violence, routine activities, social bonds, and economic deprivation, have been derived and discussed. Finally, in order to place the theoretical and conceptual approach taken here to the alcohol and homicide link in perspective, the relationship between the current approach and those of three recent and important theoretical con-tributions to the study of crime and violence has been drawn. The next task is to describe the research designs, measures, sources, and techniques to be used in the empirical testing of the implications of the material discussed in this chapter.

Chapter 3

TWO APPROACHES TO ALCOHOL AND HOMICIDE

This chapter describes the research strategies used in this study to test the implications of selective disinhibition in two macrolevel analyses of the homicide and alcohol relationship. The first analysis, the results of which are discussed in chapter 4, tests the basic implications in a longitudinal analysis of 256 cities with observations at three time points, 1960, 1970, and 1980. The second analysis, to be discussed in chapter 5, explores the way in which the selective disinhibition approach can form the basis of public policy designed to weaken or even break the alcohol and homicide link. In the latter analysis, the impact of the greatest social experiment of the 1980s (no, not the so-called Reagan Revolution), the implementation of a nearly uniform national drinking age of twenty-one years of age, on youth homicides of various types is examined in a state by time analysis. This chapter describes the units of analysis, the methodological issues and choices involved in each analysis, the statistical approaches used, and the specific measures used in the two analyses, along with references to the sources for each measure.

A LONGITUDINAL MODEL OF
CITY ALCOHOL AVAILABILITY AND HOMICIDE

As indicated previously, the first empirical analysis presented here is designed to examine the basic question of the relationship between alcohol availability and homicide rates in a large set of cities. The debate over which is the appropriate macrounit to study homicide rates with has been discussed elsewhere (Messner, 1982; Bailey, 1984; Parker, 1989; Messner and Tardiff, 1986), with the favored candidates ranging from nations (Messner, 1989) to states (Parker and Smith, 1979), metropolitan areas (Messner, 1982), counties (Parker, 1985), cities (Williams and Flewelling, 1988), to neighborhoods (Messner and Tardiff, 1986) and below. Most arguments made in this debate are reasonable: metropolitan areas are better than states because they are more homogeneous (Messner, 1982); central cities are better than metropolitan areas because homicides are concentrated in central cities (Parker, 1989); neighborhoods are better than cities because they more adequately represent the social and physical contexts in which homicides are embedded (Messner and Tardiff, 1986). None of these arguments, however, are particularly strong, and there is no one choice that a strong consensus has developed around, despite the debate having gone on for ten or more years in the literature. A few studies (Land et al., 1990; Parker, 1985) actually replicate their analyses at two or more levels, and often some differences are found, but for the most part the few studies that examine the generalizability of findings across units of analysis find more consistency than divergence.

However, more research is needed on the causes of such differences as are found, as there is no clear understanding of why such differences would occur, and whether they reflect something real in the relationships at different units or they are due simply to aggregation bias or errors. Fewer studies yet actually try to analyze multilevel models of violence (Sampson and Wooldrege, 1987), and surely more of this type of research is needed if we are to gain any more insight from these differences and similarities of findings across levels. Underlying all this debate on appropriateness, however, is the fact that this decision is also influenced by data availability, something that is not often discussed in articles and books, but is often discussed in the hallways and lounges near academic conventions.

Homicide and alcohol research has been limited to cross national studies (Lenke, 1990; Parker, 1992a; Skog, 1986), state level analyses (Parker, 1993b), or to studies of individual victims derived from medical examiner data, in which blood alcohol levels are available (see review in Murdoch et al., 1990; Welte and Abel, 1989). One of the major reasons for the lack of analyses between states and individual victims is that alcohol consumption measures are only available with national coverage and consistency at the state level, the reasons having to do in part with state level taxation and associated reporting requirements (National Institute on Alcohol Abuse and Alcoholism, 1985). A major reason for using cities in the present research is the need to address this gap. However, the selection of indicators at less than the state level dictates that availability, rather than consumption or sales of alcohol, must be the measure of choice. As discussed previously, there is a body of research that links availability consistently to consumption, and as such the lack of actual consumption or sales data is not as much of a problem as it might seem at first brush.

This still leaves the question about why *cities*, why not simply stay with *states* where the preferred measures are available, and the answer lies in part with some of the good but not overwhelming arguments mentioned previously: cities are places where the vast majority of violence occurs in the United States, and yet there is so much variation in city homicide rates that the desire to learn more about what causes such variation is strong. As to the other side of the availability argument, cities as a unit of analysis do leave the researcher access to a large number of measures collected by various offices in the United States federal government, the two principal ones being the Bureau of the Census and the Federal Bureau of Investigation. An analysis of alcohol availability and homicide at the city level is a reasonable compromise among arguments based on the logic of design on the one hand and the imperative of data availability on the other.

Theoretical Considerations:
The Importance of Multiple Perspectives

In addition to the explication of selective disinhibition and its implications for this analysis presented in chapter 2, an introduction to the other guiding theoretical approaches that provide the conceptual framework for this analysis was provided in the context of the discussion of the three interaction hypotheses to be examined. In order to appropriately represent these three theories (routine activity/lifestyle, social bonds, and economic deprivation), additional measures should also be included in the penultimate version of this model. Although including interactions, multiple theoretical approaches, and additional measures within each approach does make estimation and interpretation much more complicated (as anyone who plows their way through the technical appendices to this volume will attest to), these are a number of compelling reasons to adopt such complicated models and analyses. First, any new perspective like the selective disinhibition approach should be subjected to and survive, at least to some extent, a severe empirical test at the hands of its more established theoretical predecessors if it is to demonstrate any promise. There are so many perspectives, theories, hypotheses, and approaches to a phenomenon like violence that if we are to introduce a new one, we owe it to ourselves and the rest of the field to provide empirical evidence that the selective disinhibition has some actual value, that it adds to knowledge rather than confusion, that it actually contributes to the general understanding of violence and its causes.

It is relatively easy to select a moderate list of variables, with little or no theoretical organizing principles, and include them as controls that have been widely used in research on homicide, and end up with an inflated view of the potential contribution of selective disinhibition. It would also be easy to pick one other perspective, include its major measures, and achieve the same results. However, such research designs, along with other problems, have characterized much of the literature on homicide, and have led to "a general pattern of inconsistent results" and "many debates and publications that have resulted from...these reported inconsistencies" (both quotes from Land et al., 1990: 923). A number of analysts have recently argued for sophisticated, multiperspective models as the only hope for advancing from the tangle of contradictory findings and myriad theoretical perspectives (Land et al., 1990; Parker, 1991; 1993a; Fagan, 1990; Sampson, 1987). Such models and approaches are characterized by major complications, and these have been addressed in different ways by different analysts (Land et al., 1990; Parker, 1992b). However, there are solutions to these problems engendered by complicated models, and, as will be seen here, interesting results can arise from such efforts.

Additional Theoretical Specifications
for the City-Availability Model

In this section the additional concepts from each of the three theories to be included in the final models presented in chapter 4 are outlined. In addition, some of those ubiquitous control variables are discussed as well, so that by the time results are presented in chapter 4, the reader will have a complete index of the variables included and the rationale for each.

In addition to the inclusion of age and the interaction of age and availability discussed in chapter 2, two other measures typically derived from the routine activity measure are included in this analysis. Female labor force participation is one of the major components of Cohen and Felson's (1979) household activity ratio, a measure that has enjoyed success as a predictor of both crime and alcohol consumption (Carroll and Jackson, 1983; Treno, Parker, and Holder, 1993). In general, this theoretical approach suggests that as people spend more work and leisure time outside the home, their risk of victimization and, as such, the crime rate, goes up (Land et al., 1990: 927).

Considering female labor force participation in and of itself, however, may require a more nuanced view of the relationship between gender and routine activities. Although increased activities outside the home may expose women to more motivated offenders in the context of less effective guardianship (Cohen et al., 1981), sometimes the very guardianship that serves to protect a potential victim may in fact expose women to higher risk of homicide. Most female homicide victims are killed by males with whom they have a close, often sexually intimate, relationship (Browne and Williams, 1989; Silverman and Kennedy, 1987), and as such, more activity outside the home may actually reduce this source of homicide risk.

In addition, female labor force participation can give women greater access to economic resources, which can be translated into guardianship and other means by which homicide victimization risk can be reduced. For example, as household income from two sources increases, or as a female head of household gains labor market experience, skills, and seniority in a job, increased wages may mean access to a personal automobile for the trip to work, providing for reduced risk compared with riding public transportation and walking to and from bus stops and other locations. In addition, greater economic resources in the hands of women may allow them to protect themselves—for example, deciding to leave an abusive partner rather than remain—because greater labor force experience makes it possible to provide for children in the absence of the abusive partner (Parker, 1993a). These arguments lead to the prediction that female labor force participation may lead to less, not more, homicide, as is the typical expectation in most analyses (Gartner, 1990; Cohen et al., 1981).

A third measure derived from routine activity is also included here, retail activity associated with eating and drinking establishments. This measure is closer to the origins of this perspective in the human ecology tradition of Amos Hawley (1950), who argued that the rhythm, timing, and tempo of daily activities were essential for understanding the patterns of human interaction. This measure also focuses on an aspect of activities outside the home that, as evidenced by the homicide case studies analyzed in chapter 2, often provides a setting for homicide. Although this measure does include drinking establishments—that is, places that serve alcohol for on site consumption—the correlation of this item with the major measure of availability, the number of liquor stores (.18 for 1960; .22 for 1970, and .07 for 1980), is modest enough that rather than reflecting another aspect of alcohol availability, this measure reflects the large numbers of yogurt shops, fast food hamburger and taco places, and large chain restaurants that were built during this period. As these are all places that in general draw people from their homes, this measure should be associated with increased homicide rates.

Social Bonds: Attachments and Roots

In the discussion in chapter 2 the major indicator of social bonds was described as a composite of three indicators that reflect attachments to traditional institutions, attachment being one of the major concepts in Hirschi's (1969) formulation of social bond theory. Specifically, by combining school enrollments among the young and relatively young (ages 5 through 34), the proportion of the adult population employed, and the percent of households that have at least two members, an index of links to the institutions of family, school, and work is created.

Another aspect of social bonds would include links to other family members and others in the community, and might also include the tenure of such attachments, so that the longer one spends in such attachments, the more bonded one is to the social community. A measure available for cities that at least in part is an indicator of these larger ties and their tenure is the proportion of people in the community who have moved within the past five years. The greater the proportion of newcomers, the fewer and less meaningful the social bonds, leading to a prediction of higher homicide rates. These two measures together capture much of the attachment concept of the social bonds approach, and some aspects of the commitment and the involvement concepts. Finally, measurement of the belief concept is difficult if not impossible in a macrolevel analysis, and as such this concept has not been included here.

Economic Deprivation

This domain has included a wide variety of measures in previous research from the official poverty line measure (Messner, 1982) to infant mortality, used as an outcome of a number of processes that distinguish poverty from nonpoverty (Parker, 1989), to measures of the proportion of families who earn extremely low annual incomes (Loftin and Hill, 1974). The family structure measure used here and discussed previously in chapter 2, the proportion of children living with one parent, is also an outcome of poverty measure, in that it reflects a number of processes involving the provision of welfare, lack of employment opportunities sufficient for support of an intact family, private and local charities, the impact of divorce and out-of-wedlock births, and so on (Sampson, 1987). Two other measures that are included here also refer to aspects of this domain. As Sampson (1987) has argued so convincingly that lack of economic opportunity and the resulting breakdown in family structure explain both African-American and white rates of violence in urban areas, the proportion of the population that is African-American is used as indicator of additional aspects of poverty and lack of economic opportunity in the analysis in chapter 4 (see also Carroll and Jackson, 1983; Jackson and Carroll, 1981). In addition, median income is also included, to capture differences between cities that exist in the center of the distribution of income, rather than at the lower tail of the distribution, as the other two measures in part reflect. The higher the proportion of children living with one parent, and the higher the proportion of African-Americans in the population, the higher the homicide rate; the higher the median income, the lower the rate.

Control Variables: A Relatively Short List

Although reviews of the homicide literature contain large numbers of potential covariates (Land et al., 1990; Parker, 1991), two factors have limited the list discussed here. First, the combination of four different theoretical approaches, multiple measures from each, and the specification of interaction terms, has both made the model to be discussed in chapter 4 complicated and has resulted in a number of variables that normally end up on the controls list to have already been included for an explicit theoretical or conceptual reason. There remain two such variables that appear on almost all the variable lists of studies of homicide, population density, and a southern regional indicator. The latter indicator has a long history of controversy in homicide research, which has been thoroughly reviewed and commented on in a number of places (Land et al., 1990, Parker, 1989, both contain summaries of and references to this debate), and none of this controversy is worth discussing here. However, it seems prudent, especially for the period of time analyzed here (Parker, 1991), to include this indicator. It is also the case that controlling for this indicator may also remove a potential confounding relationship with availability, as it is the case that availability is generally lower in the southern states of the United States, as many of these states have (or did during the 1960-80 period) state monopolies on the sale of spirits or hard liquor, and on the ownership and proliferation of liquor stores (Janes and Gruenewald, 1991). Failure to control for the southern region in this case might bias the impact of the liquor store measure downward; including this indicator removes this source of potential bias from the estimate of the net effect of availability.

Finally, with regard to population density, some have seen this as a measure of the impact of crowding (Gove et al., 1979), but it could also have been seen as a measure of aggregate risk—the more dense a city, the more potential contact with motivated offenders, and the greater the homicide risk. Regardless of one's theoretical predilections, this measure is included here to control for the effect of population density independent of the other variables included.

A Longitudinal Model for Alcohol
and Homicide: 1960, 1970, and 1980

The notion that longitudinal models have a number of advantages in causal research has long been accepted, although some critics have raised issues about the efficacy of longitudinal research for each and every problem, no matter what the cost or difficulties involved (Glenn, 1981; Campbell et al., 1986; Gottfredson and Hirschi, 1990: 217-54). In fact, these latter authors give what is one of the best and most succinct statements of why a particular research design should or should not be used: "there must be an intimate connection between the conceptualization of a problem and the design of research focused on that problem" (Gottfredson and Hirschi, 1990: 252). Some have used the term *longitudinal* to refer to multiwave panel studies in which a sample of individuals is interviewed repeatedly (West and Farrington, 1977; Elliot et al., 1985). The term is used here to encompass a design that explicitly involves data collected at different times. Therefore what are traditionally referred to as time series studies (Gartner and Parker, 1990), as well as studies that consider variation in both time and space (Gartner, 1990) are considered here to be longitudinal in design. The analyses reported in chapter 4 are also longitudinal, in that the same variables are measured for the same individuals at three points in time, 1960, 1970, and 1980. The difference in this version of a panel design is that the 'individuals' are the 256 cities for which all variables previously discussed were available (a complete list of these cities is given in Appendix 2A).

What time series, pooling of overtime and cross-sectional data, and panel designs all have in common is that they are specified in recognition of the notion that the process being studied—in this case the link between alcohol and homicide—is dynamic over the time period studied—that is, past values of the measures used to understand the process have an important influence on present values and, more importantly, on estimates of present relationships among variables. If it is the case that the values of the variables considered are changing over time, and it is further the case that the relationship among variables is changing over time, then it is a fundamental misspecification to treat such data as if they were static, or cross-sectional. This line of reasoning is similar to that used by critics of longitudinal designs such as Gottfredson and Hirschi (1990:

231), who argue that the variables of primary interest in the study of individual criminality are stable over relatively long periods of time. If in fact there is no change in the system of variables specified in an analysis, longitudinal or time-inclusive research designs serve only to provide evidence of the stability of the relationships of interest. However, if there is indeed significant change over time in the variables of interest, it becomes an open question as to whether or not the relationships are static or dynamic, and only by examining these relationship over time can this important distinction be made.

The casual observer of urban America over the past several decades does not need a great deal of convincing on the issue of whether or not cities in the United States have changed, and changed in fundamental ways, during the period under consideration here. For example, the average homicide rate among the 256 cities changed from 5.34 per 100,000 in 1960, to 10.15 in 1970, to 13.76 in 1980. What accounted for this change? Even if the relationships between some of the causes of homicide that have been discussed here—like alcohol availability, poverty, social bonds, or population density have remained the same—it would be of interest to know that the increase in homicide rates between 1960 and 1980, an average change of 157 percent, was due to more poverty, greater density, or fewer social bonds. The change reflected in a comparison of mean homicide rates or mean poverty rates (our measure of poverty, children living with one parent, was 15.98 percent in 1960, 22.19 in 1970, and 32.77 in 1980) or any other variable used in this research (see Appendix 2B for descriptive information on the measures used here) is only part of the story of change or stability. Changes in the variation of these measures, and changes in the link between them in these cities, will also only be revealed if a longitudinal approach is used.

If the notion that longitudinal designs can test for change and its impact is to be taken seriously, we must utilize some rather complicated statistical methods if this process is to be adequately accounted for in an empirical model. In general, the best predictor of anything, even in the face of change, is the previous value of this anything. For example, despite the great deal of change exhibited by homicide rates in these cities between 1960 and 1980, the correlation between the 1960 city homicide rate and that for 1970 is about .64, while the equivalent 1970 to 1980 correlation is .71. However, if one translates this correlation in explained variance, a concept of doubtful utility in many cases, but illustrative here, the rate in 1960 accounts for about 41 percent of the rates in 1970, still leaving a substantial portion of the difference in rates to be explained by other factors. Even more important than this, however, is the fact that by using the past value of homicide to predict current homicide, other present predictors can now be interpreted as being related (or not, as the empirical estimates reveal) to the *change* in homicide rates between 1960 and 1970. It is also the case that the independent variables in such a model also have a similar relationship with their past values, so that once the past variation of these measures is also accounted for in a longitudinal model, we can assess the impact of change in poverty, social bonds, and so on, for the explanation of change in homicide.

Results of such models, then, provide direct estimates of the impact of stability and change in the variables of interest and allow us to see how we came to observe the current set of relationships, through the persistence or lack thereof of different effects at each time point. The degree of statistical control and precision that a longitudinal model offers for the nature of the analysis of homicide and alcohol that is the focus of this investigation surely fits the requirement of a strong and essential link between the design and the substance of the problem under study.

Structural Equation Modeling

The complexity of modeling stability and change in even a modest-sized list of variables such as have been described here requires some sophisticated statistical approach. In Appendix 1 the complete details of the approach used to estimate the three panel structural equation models, which the results discussed in chapter 4 come from, are given. However, a few general points can be made in order to further justify the use of an approach that requires a technical appendix to explain.

The main effects model, on which the basic findings on the homicide and alcohol link are based in chapter 4, involves the estimation of 23 equations, three for homicide, and one for each of the stability models linking a measure in 1960 to its counterpart in 1970 and again in 1980. For this type of model to be properly specified, the intercorrelations among variables within each time point must be estimated—that is, the relationship among independent variables that explain homicide at each time point. This results in just under two hundred parameters to be specified and estimated. Structural equation modeling techniques make it possible to plan and execute such an analysis, and doing so within this statistical framework has some advantages. First, because the 23 equations and associate parameters are estimated simultaneously, rather than as 23 separate regression equations, the efficiency gained results in better, read smaller, estimates of standard errors, which means a better chance of detecting an effect that is, in the population, statistically significant. In addition, simultaneously estimating all the equations allows for the detection and estimation of effects not anticipated by theory—that is, the final model is both deductive and inductive in origin. This is an advantage, as some of these relationships, however trivial they may be from a theoretical point of view, may have an impact on the estimate of more important relationships in the model.

For example, one of these effects that was detected in the early stages of model estimation was that female labor force participation in 1970 had a significant effect on retail eating and drinking establishment activity per capita in 1970, in addition to the significant impact of eating and drinking establishment activity in 1960. Accounting for such sources of variation in the independent variables has an impact on the estimate of the relationship between these variables and homicide rates. To fail to specify such effects results in biased estimates, upwardly biased, of the impact of these variables on homicide rates. Although some of the effects included in the final model (given in Appendix 1) are not easily understood as this example, no effect was specified where it was nonsensical to do so. Ignoring these effects results in misspecification, including them leads to a complicated model.

As implied by the previous discussion, structural equation computer programs (EQS/Windows, version 4 [Bentler and Wu, 1993], running on a variety of 486 and [very slowly] 386 personal computers) provide diagnostic information concerning the overall fit of the model estimated and the places in the model that can be changed to improve fit, as well as the standard information required to report explained variances and tests of significance of individual coefficients. It is also relatively easy to specify correlations among errors in equations, a task that is required in the time-inclusive models discussed here. Some of what makes the previous value of a variable the current value's best predictor are common sources of error that need to be accounted for in this type of analysis. Once again, failure to specify these autocorrelation effects leads to upwardly biased estimates.

Interaction Models

The specification of the three interactions to be tested—social bonds, poverty, and routine activity—all with alcohol availability, can also be incorporated into the structural equation model described here. The specific form of these interactions to be used here is one in which, with the main effects present in the equation, terms constructed to represent the combined effect of the two variables are entered into the model at each time point, and analyzed in the same way as any variable, with stability equations across time, within time covariances with other measures, including the main effects, and effect estimates in the homicide equations at each time point. Interaction effects are often very difficult to detect, and they can also contribute to estimation problems like multicolinearity (Land et al., 1990, on the general problem of multicolinearity in homicide research). However, there are different ways to specify interactions, and the approach used here tends to minimize multicolinearity problems at the expense of some precision. The choice of approaches really depends, like the choice of longitudinal or cross-sectional models, on the nature of the prediction being made. As was discussed in chapter 2, the three interactions predicted to affect homicide are ones in which the impact of extremely high alcohol availability enhances or strengthens the impact of the three measures.

For example, if the younger the median age, the higher the homicide rate, the prediction is that in places with below average median ages, high levels of alcohol availability would be particularly effective at increasing homicide rates. If age had only a main effect on homicide, it would not matter at what particular point on the line that represents the relationship between median age and homicide one examined, the strength of the relationship would be constant over the range of the two variables. This interaction hypothesis, however, suggests that at the low end of the relationship, the connection between median age and homicide is stronger when high availability is also present. One way to capture this combination of the tails of age and availability is to construct dummy variables, measuring each city as to whether it belongs to the extreme as to median age or availability, and then to multiply the two dummy indicators together so that the resulting variable equals one only when a city has both a very young population and very high availability.

The situation with the other two interactions is similar. Like the case for median age, the case for social bonds suggests that homicide would be highest when attachments to school, work, and home are fewest, and the impact of availability is thought to exacerbate this relationship when availability is particularly high. A low bonds dummy was constructed and multiplied by the very high availability dummy described previously. Poverty, as measured here by the proportion of children living with one parent, was also used to form an above average indicator for the higher range of poverty in a city, and again combined with the very high availability dummy. In each case, with the exception of median age, the indicators were formed by assigning a one to cities that were more than one standard deviation above or below the mean on the continuous variable. The distribution of median age was such that the indicator was constructed as any city that was below the average median age in the sample.

The reason that these interaction terms help to minimize the impact of collinearity is that they represent only a certain portion of the two main effects indicators. In the case of a multiplicative interaction term, in which the expected interaction effect exists across the entire range of both variables, collinearity will be much greater, because each variable's range is represented twice in the equation, once in the main effect and once in the interaction term. If the interaction is clear, however, this collinearity will not prevent the effect from being significant. Here the prediction is for the interaction to occur at a specific point or subrange along the distribution of the two variables, and using this approach also has the benefit of minimizing estimation problems.

How Can the Alcohol/Homicide
Link be Broken: A Policy Analysis

Until this point in the present study, little has been said about the second analysis to be discussed in chapter 5. Earlier in this chapter, this policy-based analysis was briefly described, and it is now appropriate, before discussing the measures and sources of data for all the analyses reported here, to describe in greater detail the specification of an analysis that assesses the impact of increased minimum legal drinking ages on youth homicide that occurred during the decade of the 1980s. If the theoretical reasoning in chapter 2 is supported by results in chapter 4 that indicate the importance of alcohol for our understanding of homicide (which I can assure the reader is the case), the question of interest can shift to a focus on how to reduce the impact of alcohol on homicide. The advent of increased minimum age of purchase laws provides an excellent opportunity to evaluate how interventions designed to have an impact of consumption may also have an impact on homicide, and the purpose of this second analysis is to address this possibility.

Conceptual Framework: Why Minimum
Purchase Laws Would Have an Effect

An increase in the minimum age for purchasing alcohol is likely to have a significant but limited impact on homicide. At first consideration it would be logical to assume that this impact would be limited to those directly affected by the change—that is, individuals who were 18, 19, and 20 years old when the change occurs. Although some states included grandfather clauses in the statute that raised the minimum age of purchase (O'Malley and Wagenaar, 1991), most did not, and those in this age group went from having legal access to being denied legal access, in some cases for up to three additional years. Further consideration, especially of the social aspects of such laws and the individuals affected by them, suggests that individuals both slightly above the new minimum age (21) and those slightly below the previous minimum (18) might also be affected by the change. If the minimum is 18 years old, many individuals in the 15-17 year-old group will have contact with 18 year olds who can legally purchase alcohol. On the other hand, those individuals who are denied legal access until aged 21 have, by the time they reach legal age, a different set of experiences and expectancies with regard to alcohol consumption. Studies of the onset of drinking show that individuals who begin drinking later have different consumption patterns—that is, more moderate—than those who begin drinking at earlier ages (Saltz and Elandt, 1986). So both through its impact on availability and consumption, and on its broader social effects, minimum age of purchases increases could have an impact on homicide rates.

However, such an effect would be unlikely to be relevant to the entire spectrum of homicide. In addition to the obvious link to the age of victims and offenders (offenders and victims, especially those aged 15 through 24, tend to be similar on a number of demographic characteristics, but particularly on age; Lauretsen et al., 1991), previous research on the impact of prior victim-offender relationships also suggests that the impact of minimum age of purchase increases would be stronger for primary homicides, or those in which the victim and offender knew each other prior to the homicide, than would be the case for nonprimary homicides, in which the police were unable to find any prior connection between the victim and the offender (Parker, 1989). Selective disinhibition would also seem to be more relevant for primary homicides, as there are many more opportunities for disputes between people who know each other and spend considerable time together, and it may be more likely in such situations that active constraint is what keeps homicide from occurring. If alcohol helps individuals to overcome active constraint, then limiting the access to availability and consumption of alcohol for young people may have preventive effects on youth homicide.

Specification of a Policy-Impact Analysis:
Additional Factors to be Considered

As was the case for the analyses of alcohol and homicide in general, an adequate examination of this line of reasoning linking minimum purchase age to youth homicide can be done only in the presence of addition variables that might also impact youth homicide. The most important of these, especially in the context of this effort, is alcohol consumption itself. Unlike availability, which has been directly tied to aggregate consumption of alcohol, the use of minimum age of purchase as the sole proxy for consumption is more problematic. First, it may be the case that consumption among people aged 15 through 20 is a relatively small portion of the total level of consumption. Some have used the age range 20-29 to represent high consumption, a fact that further underscores the notion that minimum age of purchase is not the best consumption proxy (Treno, Parker, and Holder, 1993). In addition, lax enforcement of higher minimum age of purchase may also undermine this measure as a proxy for consumption. However, the existence of the higher minimum age does increase opportunity costs for underage drinkers seeking to purchase alcohol, and it may cause some alcohol providers to increase vigilance, especially near the beginning of the time after the change has been implemented. It therefore makes sense to include both consumption and the minimum age of purchase laws in this analysis of youth homicide, both because of the fact that minimum age of purchase indicators may measure things other than consumption and because consumption, for a number of reasons already discussed here, may have a direct effect on homicide among youth.

Due to the nature of this analysis, a more limited set of additional variables is included in the final model. Income inequality, which has a somewhat checkered past in homicide research in general, has been included here (Blau and Blau, 1982; Williams, 1984; Messner and Tardiff, 1986). Economic inequality could help create situations in which violence may seem a useful alternative, thus leading to situations in which selective disinhibition could occur. Infant mortality is included as a measure of poverty (Loftin and Hill, 1974; Loftin and Parker, 1985; Parker, 1989), and racial composition is included, in line with arguments previously discussed. Finally, a southern regional indicator and total population are included in order to serve as proxies for a number of potential effects.

RESEARCH DESIGN OF THE POLICY-IMPACT STUDY: ANOTHER LONGITUDINAL APPROACH

The explanation for the rather abbreviated list of predictors included in the minimum age of purchase and youth homicide can be found in the nature of the design required to evaluate the impact of this intervention. There are a number of features of this analysis that require a very different sort of design than that used in the analysis of availability and homicide. First, and most important, the nature of the intervention is such that it can occur in any of the fifty states plus the District of Columbia at any time, so that the requirement of a dynamic model is again met, but in this case any number of states may pass the new higher minimum age of purchase in any particular year, so the appropriate design must be able to measure a number of impacts in any particular year. In most cases the laws passed during the 1980s took effect quickly, and any design that hoped to capture the impact of this intervention would have to include frequent measurement across all 51 units. A longitudinal design that combines data from cross sections measured repeatedly, referred to as pooled cross-section time series analysis (Stimson, 1985; Saffer and Grossman, 1987; Gartner, 1990), is one that again meets the criteria discussed previously concerning the fit between the conceptualization of the problem at hand and the design to be employed.

This approach first of all solves the problem of evaluating the impact of what is a number of single interventions, taking effect in a relatively short period of time, by treating each intersection of time and one of the 51 states as a possible realization of the intervention. This means that cases and time periods can be combined, because each observation in the matrix defined by the intersection of state with time period is a possible site for evaluating the impact of this intervention. The data to be examined here cover the period 1976 through 1983, so that if each state were to be considered separately, the maximum amount of time we could examine for the impact of the intervention is seven years, given that Minnesota was the first state to raise the minimum age of purchase to 21, in 1977 (O'Malley and Wagenaar, 1991). However, if we combine states by time periods, we have 408 (51 by 8) opportunities to look for the impact of this intervention. Normally we must assume that these realizations of the process are independent, clearly not the case in the pooled design, but because this design has received a great deal of attention in the research literature, the problems are well understood and the solutions are available and accessible (Nerlove, 1971; Maddala, 1971; Stimson, 1985).

The requirement of frequent measurement, in this case yearly, restricts the number of independent variables that can be considered, most of which are measured every ten, or in a few cases every five, years in the course of large-scale census bureau efforts. On the other hand, computerized versions of the Supplemental Homicide Report (FBI, 1987) provide greater detail on homicide than is available for data going back to 1960, as is included in the previously described analysis. This detail allows for the classification of homicide into primary and nonprimary rates.

Summary of the Research Designs Employed
to Examine Alcohol and Homicide

The two studies that have been described here are different in a number of ways, but they share common elements and are complementary in at least one important manner. Among the common elements they share is the explicit recognition of the dynamic aspects of both the basic alcohol availability and homicide analyses, and the policy-impact analysis of minimum age of purchase and youth homicide model. The most important feature in common, however, is the important role that alcohol plays in both analyses, at least according to the underlying conceptual models that have been used to specify each analysis. The fact that the units of analysis are different, and the time periods analyzed only overlap to the smallest degree help to make the two studies complementary. Each can serve to validate the other as to the major premise of both: the central role that alcohol plays in the explanation of homicide rates.

Measures Used and Sources of Data

In the analyses of city homicide rates and alcohol availability, the following measures and sources were used.

Homicide rate per 100,000 population: These data are for the years 1963, 1972, and 1982, and are reported in the annual publication, *Uniform Crime Report*, published by the Federal Bureau of Investigation. The appropriate years are 1964, 1973, and 1983, as the report is published in the following year to which the data pertain, usually during the fall.

Alcohol availability: This variable, the number of liquor stores per 1,000 population, is also measured for 1963, 1972, and 1982, and was taken from the *Census of Business*, Retail Trade section, which was published by the U.S. Bureau of the Census in 1963, 1974, and 1982.

All the remaining variables used in this analysis are from the *City and County Data Book Consolidated File*, a consolidated longitudinal computer file first issued in 1978 by the Bureau of the Census and updated in 1983 to include 1980 census data; each variable is measured in 1960, 1970, and 1980.

Age: the median age of the city population

Racial Composition: percent of the population that was African-American

Social Bonds: This measure is a composite of the z scores of three indicators; percent of the population aged 5-24 enrolled in school, percent of the population living in households having two or more members, and percent of the population employed.

Southern regional indicator: A value of one (zero was assigned to cities in other regions) was assigned to cities located in states that were members of the confederacy of states that seceded from the federal union in 1860 and 1861.

Population density: population per square mile

Female labor force participation: percent of the labor force that is female

Retail eating and drinking activity: annual expenditures per capita on retail eating and drinking establishments, with 1960 and 1970 values converted to 1980 dollars

Income: median family income, with each of the three measures expressed in 1980 dollars

Migration: the percent of the city population over the age of five who have moved (defined as crossing a county line or further) in the last five years

Children with one parent: percent of population under 18 years old who live with one parent

All of these variables are measured at the city level.

———————

Interaction terms were based on the multiplication of the following components:

High availability: assigned a value of one if the number of liquor stores per 1,000 population was more than one standard deviation above the mean level for the sample of cities within each year of measurement (see Appendix 2B for descriptive statistics and correlations)

Young median age: assigned a value of one if the median age was below the average median age for the sample of cities within each year

Low social bonds: assigned a value of one if the score on the composite bonds measure was more than one standard deviation below the mean for the sample of cities within each year

High poverty: assigned a value of one if the percent of children living with one parent was more than one standard deviation above the mean for the sample of cities within each year.

Sources and Measures for the Policy Analysis

Homicide rates: for each state and single year, 1976 through 1983, rate of primary and nonprimary homicide for victims aged 15-18, 19-20, and 21-24, per 100,000 population

Inequality: based on two time points during the 1976-83 period, 1976 and 1980. Measured by taking the difference between the percent of families earning more than $50,000 and the percent of families earning less than $10,000. The data for each state, 1976, were taken from the *Current Population Reports*, series P-60, published in 1977; and for 1980, from the *Census of the Population*, vol. 1, published in 1983, both by the Bureau of the Census.

Poverty: measured by the infant mortality rate, and available in National Center for Health Statistics, *Vital Statistics of the U.S.*, vol. 2, *Mortality* (1977-84), published annually

Alcohol consumption: measured as beer consumption, in barrels per capita, from *The Brewing Industry in the U.S.: The Brewer's Almanac*, complied by P.C. Katz, and published in 1986 by the Beer Institute, Washington, D.C.

Minimum age change: assigned a value of one in the year in which the minimum age of purchase for alcohol was increased at least one year of age over the previous legal minimum; taken from O'Malley and Wagenaar, 1991. During the period included here, 1976-83, nineteen states increased the minimum age of purchase.

Racial composition: proportion nonwhite, from the *Current Population Reports*, series P-25, published annually, 1977-80, 1982-84, and for 1980, from the *Census of the Population*, vol. 1, published in 1983, both by the Bureau of the Census.

Southern regional indicator: measured as previously described for each state

Total Population: taken from the *Current Population Reports*, series P-25; published annually, 1977-80, 1982-84, and for 1980, from the *Census of the Population*, vol. 1, published in 1983, both by the Bureau of the Census.

Chapter 4

Results of Longitudinal Analyses of City Homicide Rates

The results of the longitudinal analyses of city alcohol availability and homicide rates are presented and discussed in this chapter, as well as the results of three analyses in which interactions between high alcohol availability and indicators of poverty, routine activity, and social bonds. Figure 4.1 gives the general form of these models, and before presenting the results some aspects of figure 4.1 should be highlighted.

One of the advantages of a true longitudinal model (Greenberg and Kessler, 1982) is that it provides insight into both stability and change in the variables and relationships included in the model. The paths in figure 4.1 that go from the 1960 independent variables such as female labor force participation, city alcohol availability, and so on, are the stability estimates. If availability in all 256 cities in the database had remained unchanged between 1960 and 1970, the standardized coefficient for the stability estimate would be 1.00. Anything less than 1.00 indicates that some change took place between 1960 and 1970. The additional advantage of estimating

FIGURE 4.1
Conceptual Model

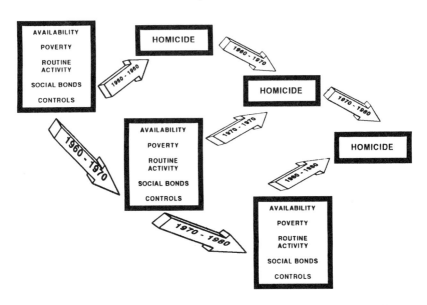

these stability parameters is that when the effect of 1970 availability or median age on homicide is estimated, the resulting parameter represents the impact of the change in availability or median age between 1960 and 1970 on homicide in 1970. If the same specification is applied to the dependent variable, so that the stability estimate of homicide between 1960 and 1970 is specified, then the parameter estimate from availability or median age to homicide can be interpreted as the impact of changes in availability or median age on changes in homicide. So this type of specification can truly address issues of stability and change in the relationships between homicide, alcohol availability, and the remaining variables in the model.

It should be noted that any significant effects found at the 1970 and 1980 stages of the model should be considered more important than those found for the base line period, or 1960, precisely because of the stricter degree of control afforded by this type of model when prior levels of the dependent and independent variables are included. When examining the 1960 results, for example, we cannot know whether a particular parameter that is significant would be so if the previous values of both variables in the relationship being estimated had been available for inclusion in the model. These base line results are useful, important, and are of interest to the evaluation of hypotheses concerning the impact of alcohol on homicide, and they are as valid as any standard analysis. However, any significant results that survive the stricter controls of the stability and change model should be considered very seriously in terms of their implications for the hypotheses tested here.

The model shown in figure 4.1 is comprehensive, so that a number of important theoretical perspectives are represented. This type of model, despite the complexities involved, has been of increasing interest to those who study homicide and its causes (Parker, 1989; Gartner, 1990; Land et al., 1990). The study of homicide has reached the stage in which a number of reasonably well-specified theories have been advanced, and each has generated some empirical support. To advance theoretically, we need to have more information concerning the overlap or independence of the processes identified in these theories. The only way to gain such information is to contrast multiple theories in the same model (Parker, 1991). Finally, estimating the various equations in the model shown in figure 4.1 would be difficult to achieve without the use of state of the art structural equation modeling techniques. Each equation could be estimated separately, with residuals calculated and used in later steps of the model, but the overall effects of considering stability and change simultaneously yields statistical efficiencies (smaller standard errors as previously discussed), as well as more effective statistical control.

The results presented in this chapter were estimated with EQS for Windows (version 4) running on two different personal computers: 486 33 megahertz machine and a 386 16 megahertz machine. Estimation times ranged from 20 to 35 minutes on the faster computer, and 8 to 12 hours on the slower one: these times include estimation of parameters and computation of diagnostics. Results for each of the four models—main effects and the three interaction models—are presented in two tables, the first giving the metric or unstandardized coefficients, standard errors, significance tests (a two-tailed .05 significance level was used for all tests), explained variances, and overall model-fit statistics. The second table gives the standardized coefficients.

CITY AVAILABILITY AND HOMICIDE:
THE MAIN EFFECTS MODEL

The overall model-fit statistics for the main effects model, given at the bottom of table 4.1, show that the model fits modestly well. The technical details of model fitting as used here are described in Appendix 1. Here it is sufficient to say that an initial model was estimated, diagnostic information was examined, and additional parameters having nothing to do with the substance of this analysis were added to the model until a reasonable fit of the sort shown in table 4.1 was obtained. This process requires a number of iterations, but it is important to note that over the last five iterations, the results given here and in the following tables were robust to the changes introduced to improve model-fit. It is possible that fit could be improved further, and, as described in Appendix 1, attempts were made to do so, but these attempts resulted in no great improvement in overall fit nor any substantive changes in the findings. The criteria of robustness and no important changes in model-fit constitute reasonable stopping rules in structural equation modeling.

The conclusion of reasonable fit for the model given in table 4.1 is based on the chi-square statistic; although it is just over three times the number of degrees of freedom, and therefore could be considered in the technical sense as significant—that is, the expected relationships generated from the estimated parameters in the model are still some distance from the observed relationships represented by the covariance matrix that was used as input—the chi-square value reported in table 4.1 is well below that of the original, unmodified estimated model. The chi-square value for that model was 3140.62, with 321 degrees of freedom. The process of model fitting has, therefore, significantly improved the overall fit—3140.62 − 977.72 = 2162.90—distributed as chi-square with 21 degrees of freedom. In addition, the comparative fit index (Bentler, 1990) is nearly equal to .95, which is considered an appropriate value for a reasonably well-fitting model.

The major factors that were found to significantly predict homicide rates in 1960 were female labor force participation, social bonds, migration, racial composition, and the southern regional indicator. Some of these findings are consistent with a number of other studies of homicide, and serve to validate the approach used here as a sort of base line for the rest of the model. For example, a number of studies

TABLE 4.1
City Availability and Homicide Rates,
Metric Coefficients and Standard Errors

Variables	1960	1970	1980
Alcohol availability	0.874[a]	4.698*	-3.098
	1.131[b]	2.682	3.244
Female labor force participation	-0.307*	-0.271*	-1.002*
	0.079	0.103	0.211
Median age	0.139	0.230	-0.058
	0.076	0.173	0.141
Retail eating/drinking establishments	0.008	-0.010	0.038
	0.017	0.014	0.020
Children with one parent	0.037	0.029	0.066
	0.091	0.071	0.094
Social bonds composite	-0.513*	0.018	-0.315
	0.251	0.268	0.452
Migration	0.115*	0.065	0.131*
	0.031	0.040	0.058
Median family income	-0.205	0.016	-0.154
	0.114	0.099	0.148
Population density	0.029	0.043	0.180
	0.050	0.052	0.097
Racial composition	0.162*	0.332*	0.194*
	0.037	0.038	0.058
Southern region	1.916*	0.308	-1.037
	0.684	0.799	1.104
Homicide 1960		0.383*	
		0.068	
Homicide 1970			0.605*
			0.010
Explained variance	0.473	0.644	0.601

Model Fit:

chi-square = 977.72   df = 300   fit index = .949
[a] = metric coefficient   [b] = standard error   * = significant effect

have found racial composition and the southern indicator significant for studies of 1960 homicide rates (Loftin and Hill, 1974; Parker
and Smith, 1979; Land et al., 1990). In addition, a number of analyses
have revealed that measures derived from social bonds, like the composite used here and the migration variable, are significant net predictors of crime and delinquency at the individual level (Liska and
Reed, 1985; Byrne and Sampson, 1984; Krohn and Massey, 1980).

The finding that female labor force participation has a significant and negative effect on city homicide rates is somewhat unusual,
however. Both prior research and theoretical reasoning from the routine activity/lifestyle approach would suggest that increases in
female labor force participation would be related to increased risk of
homicide (Gartner, 1990; Cohen and Felson, 1979). On the other
hand, it is clear that routine activity was derived as a uniform theory
of crime—that is, it does not differentiate by type of crime, or, in the
case of homicide, by subtype. Especially with regard to the homicide
risk experienced by women, it is clear that routine activity theory
does not consider the possibility that those who would normally be
considered capable guardians within that theory—for example, other
family members, especially male spouses, and others who have close
and intimate relationships with female members of the household—
may also be motivated offenders. One explanation for this negative
effect on homicide is that increased participation in work outside the
home on the part of women may in fact reduce their risk of homicide, because the vast majority of women who are victims of homicide are killed by men in their own household or men who have (or
have had in the past) close and intimate relationships with their
female victims—spouses, boyfriends, ex-lovers (Silverman and
Kennedy, 1987; Browne and Williams, 1989). By working outside
the home, then, women in fact may be reducing their exposure to
motivated offenders, in terms of routine activity theory.

A second explanation that may contribute to the reduced risk
experienced by women who work outside the home is the fact that
doing so increases the resources that women have to, if you will,
purchase additional guardianship, in terms of living arrangements,
mode of transportation—that is, private auto versus public transit,
and so on. Women who experience victimization at the hands of a
significant other may be able, under a situation in which such individuals are active participants in the labor market, to relocate away
from the threatening significant other. Women who are not active in

the labor market may have fewer options in such a situation (Parker, 1993a). Regardless of the explanation for this finding, it does seem that routine activity would benefit from an attempt to specify more precisely expectations about how indicators like female labor force participation would affect subtypes of homicide and other violent crimes (Parker, 1992b; Parker and Toth, 1990; Parker, 1989).

When consideration is directed toward the 1970 results, the first benefits of both the theoretical infusion of alcohol into a model of homicide and the superior control afforded by a longitudinal model become apparent. City alcohol availability has a significant net effect on 1970 homicide rates. In addition to being consistent with the logic of selective disinhibition, the fact that availability is found to be significant for 1970 and not for either 1960 or 1980 can be understood in terms of the trends in alcohol consumption and the nature of the variable itself. As will be recalled, this measure is based on a census of liquor stores, which are places, depending on the state alcohol beverage control scheme, that sell several types of alcoholic beverages.

However, what all liquor stores have in common is that they sell distilled spirits. Figure 4.2 gives the trend in distilled spirits consumption in the United States between 1950 and 1986. What is

FIGURE 4.2
Spirits Consumption, 1950-86

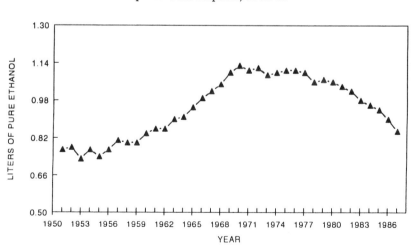

particularly interesting for the explanation of the findings in table 4.1 is that during the 1960s, spirits consumption jumped dramatically, increasing more than 30 percent between 1960 and 1969, when consumption peaked at 1.13 gallons of pure alcohol equivalent per capita. Figure 4.2 also offers an explanation as to why the effect did not persist: between 1969 and 1980, spirits consumption dropped steadily while homicide rates were increasing. This does not mean that during the 1970s and beyond alcohol can be assumed to have no impact on homicide. The fact that only one major type of beverage is being well represented by the measure used here, as well as results to be discussed in chapter 5 where beer consumption is used as an indicator, both suggest otherwise. It does seem clear, however, that the increase in spirits consumption during the 1960s had something to do with the increase in homicide. Other research has also linked spirits consumption to violence in a similar manner (Room, 1989; Murdoch and Pihl, 1988). The fact that this effect is found net of prior homicide is further support for the conclusion that availability had an important influence on homicide in the 1970s.

The results for 1970 reveal some additional findings of interest, with female labor force having a similar net impact on homicide in 1970 as it did on homicide in 1960. Racial composition is the only other variable from the list of significant effects in 1960 that is also significant in 1970. Among the list of factors that were significant in 1960 that are not for 1970, the southern regional indicator is the most interesting. A number of static analyses have found this variable to be significant for circa 1970 homicide rates (Parker, 1989; Land et al., 1990), but it is clear from the results in table 4.1 that this is largely a reflection of an effect from the previous time periods. Once the focus is put on change, it becomes clear that nonsouthern homicide rates were growing during the 1960s and 1970s, and the unique position of the region vis-à-vis homicide was eroding, so that by the mid-1980s the western region, rather than the southern region, recorded the highest regional homicide rates (Parker, 1994a: 146-47).

Results for 1980 continue to show the importance of control and a dynamic approach. Female labor force participation and racial composition continue to have significant effects, joined by migration, as in 1960. Although remaining insignificant, the effect of the southern region on homicide in 1980 actually turns negative, a finding that will be discussed in greater detail below.

Table 4.2 gives the standardized coefficients, an examination of which shows the dominance of racial composition and female labor force participation in all three equations. The impact of migration is important in 1960, and more modest in 1980, with the availability effect in 1970 being modest, the smallest of the significant effects in that equation. By 1980 the effect of racial composition has diminished substantially, but remains the highest standardized coefficient in the 1980 equation, followed by female labor force participation.

Overall, the findings of the main effects model of city availability and homicide show modest support for the macrolevel implications of selective disinhibition. It is particularly important that the significant effect of availability on homicide is for 1970, as the design of model provides a stricter standard of proof for the 1970 and 1980 results. Two other findings stand out in these results: the consistent negative impact of female labor force participation, and the absence of a significant effect for the southern regional indicator

TABLE 4.2
City Availability and Homicide Rates, Standardized Coefficients

Variables	1960	1970	1980
Alcohol availability	0.037	0.091	-0.040
Female labor force participation	-0.253	-0.115	-0.252
Median age	0.135	0.146	-0.023
Retail eating/drinking establishments	0.031	-0.031	0.098
Children with one parent	0.051	0.029	0.065
Social bonds composite	-0.134	0.003	-0.042
Migration	0.230	0.074	0.118
Median family income	-0.146	0.009	-0.071
Population density	0.029	0.028	0.078
Racial composition	0.458	0.620	0.331
Southern region	0.210	0.021	-0.056
Homicide 1960		0.239	
Homicide 1970			0.473

after the initial base line equation. Once additional controls for stability as well as change are introduced, the impact of the southern region disappears. Both these findings distinguish this research from a number of studies previously cited here, and they demonstrate the importance of considering both static and dynamic aspects of homicide and the causes of homicide.

There has been an accumulation of evidence that the unique impact of the south on homicide, which was seen to be related to the historical construction of the underlying link between alcohol and violence in chapter 2, was at best overestimated in a few oft cited studies (Hackney, 1968; Gastil, 1971)—as was originally argued by Loftin and Hill (1974)—with a number of static studies contributing to this notion (Parker and Smith, 1979; Smith and Parker, 1980; DeFranzo, 1983; Bailey, 1984; Jackson, 1984; Williams, 1984; Loftin and Parker, 1985; Williams and Flewelling, 1988; Parker, 1989). However, this notion persists in the literature, again with static studies finding an effect of the southern region similar to that found here for 1960 (Messner, 1982, 1983a; Rosenfeld, 1986; Blau and Golden, 1986; Huff-Corzine et al., 1986; Land et al., 1990), albeit the list in favor of the southern hypothesis seems to be shorter than those opposed. The results in table 4.1 may serve as a challenge to those who support this hypothesis to provide a stricter test of the impact of the south on homicide rates through the specification of dynamic models. If this is undertaken by a number of analysts, we may finally be able to put this hypothesis to rest.

There is little disagreement in the research literature with regard to the consistent impact that racial composition has on homicide rates. The current study only confirms this finding in the context of a dynamic model. The controversy about this effect is in the meaning attached to it by various theoretical approaches, although both the best theoretical arguments and the best data, both advanced by Sampson (1987), strongly suggest that racial composition is a surrogate for a number of important effects of economic inequality, poverty, and subsequent family disruption that have concentrated impact on the African-American population in the United States (see also Wilson, 1987).

Finally, the strong and consistent negative relationship between female labor force participation and homicide suggests that some theoretical revisions are in order for the routine activity perspective. Although this perspective has in general been quite successful in garnering empirical support in a number of studies of homicide (Parker, 1989; Parker and Toth, 1990; Messner and Tardiff, 1985), the larger number of supporting results have come from studies of crime other than homicide, studies that have used the National Crime Victimization Survey (NCVS) or have adopted the victimization instrument from the NCVS (U.S. Bureau of Justice Statistics, 1992; Miethe et al., 1987). It may be the case that homicide requires some additional theoretical analysis, especially that which would consider the role of gender interaction in homicide, if these findings are to be reconciled with the general theoretical model of routine activity. This interpretation is consistent with a finding presented in Parker (1992b), in which a ratio of on-site consumption alcohol beverage establishments is negatively related to a type of homicide in which both victim and offender are family members. That finding may also be understood in terms of an interaction by gender in the impact that outside the home activities have in either reducing or enhancing risk of violent victimization.

Interaction Model #1: Poverty, Availability, and City Homicide Rates

Tables 4.3 and 4.4 present the results of the first interaction model, in which the main effects model is reestimated with an additional term at each time point, that being a composite of places that have above average rates of children living with only one parent, the indicator of poverty used in this study, and very high levels of city alcohol availability—that is, places with rates of availability more than one standard deviation above the mean for the entire 256 city sample. The resulting model does not fit the data as well as that given in table 4.1. As the bottom panel of table 4.3 shows, the introduction of the interaction terms has resulted in an increase of 65 degrees of freedom; if the inclusion of these additional variables had no impact on model fit, the chi-square would have increased by about 65. The chi-square for the first interaction model, however, is nearly two hundred points higher than that given at the bottom of table 4.1. Examination of the diagnostics did not reveal any new path to better model fit that had not already been examined and found wanting in the main effects model. To keep the interaction models comparable to the main effects model, no additional changes were introduced. However, fitting the interactions from the equivalent base line model was con-

TABLE 4.3
Availability and Poverty Interaction Effects,
Metric Coefficients and Standard Errors

Variables	1960	1970	1980
Alcohol availability	0.327[a]	2.247	-1.423
	1.363[b]	2.034	3.698
Female labor force participation	-0.304*	-0.268*	-1.011*
	0.078	0.106	0.211
Median age	0.148	0.230	-0.052
	0.076	0.175	0.140
Retail eating/drinking establishments	0.013	-0.009	0.038*
	0.017	0.014	0.019
Children with one parent	0.011	0.025	0.065
	0.091	0.071	0.094
Social nonds composite	-0.509*	0.015	-0.322
	0.251	0.277	0.451
Migration	0.119*	0.066	0.133*
	0.031	0.040	0.058
Median family income	-0.223*	0.013	-0.159
	0.111	0.101	0.148
Population density	0.035	0.055	0.192*
	0.051	0.054	0.097
Racial composition	0.173*	0.331*	0.200*
	0.037	0.038	0.058
Southern region	1.906*	0.207	-1.039
	0.686	0.796	1.100
One parent/high availability	-0.020	1.706*	-1.194
	0.936	0.868	1.377
Homicide 1960		0.389*	
		0.070	
Homicide 1970			0.602*
			0.079
Explained variance	0.475	0.654	0.602

chi-square = 1159.22   df = 365   fit index = .942
[a] = metric coefficient   [b]= standard error   * = significant effect

ducted as a validity check, and in each of the three models the same adjustments were made to reach the best fit as was the case for the main effects model. This should not be surprising to the student of structural equation modeling, for the differences between the inter-action models and the main effects model are slight, given that only three new variables are included, and these themselves are combina-tions of variables already in the main effects model. The goodness of fit index declines only slightly, from .949 in table 4.1 to .942 in table 4.3. The explained variances are slightly larger than those in table 4.1, as would be expected when an additional variable is added to each equation. This is particularly the case for the 1970 equation, with the reason being apparent from the results in tables 4.3 and 4.4, which will be discussed in greater detail next.

Like the results discussed previously, female labor force and racial composition have strong and consistent effects that are not altered by the inclusion of the poverty/availability interaction term. Findings for migration and social bonds are also similar across the three time periods, as compared to those in the main effects model, as is the finding that the southern region has no significant impact on homicide in 1970 and 1980. However, there are also a number of interesting differences in all three time periods.

In the 1960 equation, the inclusion of the interaction term, focusing on the more extreme end of the poverty continuum, has the effect of further distinguishing the role of median income, a measure more reflective of the middle of the income distribution than either the upper, affluent range or the lower, poverty range (Loftin and Parker, 1985). In table 4.3, median family income has a significant and negative effect on homicide, as would be expected from an eco-nomic deprivation perspective. Even though the interaction term itself is nonsignificant, the inclusion of this new term in the equa-tion has an important outcome, a fact that argues against a modeling strategy in which initial models are estimated, and only significant effects are reestimated for the final model. One of the most impor-tant aspects of control is to discover what impact including a vari-able, even if that variable itself seems to have no direct effect on homicide, on the other important predictors in the model. With the impact of the poverty and availability interaction controlled for, the negative impact of median income on homicide is significant.

The results in table 4.3 for 1970 are even more important for the central premise of this study. Compared with the main effects model, the results here are similar in that female labor force, racial composition, and 1960 homicide are all significant, and, as table 4.4 shows, are the three most important predictors of homicide in 1970. However, the introduction of the interaction term has rendered the main effect of availability insignificant, but the interaction of poverty and availability is significant, net of all the other variables in the equation. Places that have the combination of both high rates of availability and an above average percentage of children living with only one parent have significantly higher homicide rates than places that have one or the other of these conditions, or neither of these conditions. Once again the fact that this effect is found in the 1970 equation gives it greater weight than would be the case if it were found in the 1960 equation, due to the stricter test that the dynamic specification used here provides.

The results for 1980 are less interesting with regard to the inter-action term, which is found to be statistically insignificant. On the other hand, like the case for 1960, controlling for this interaction has had some impact on these results. For example, the routine activity measure, retail eating and drinking activity, is a significant predictor of homicide in 1980, a finding that is consistent with the general pre-diction from routine activity that more exposure outside the home results in greater risk of homicide. In addition, population density is also significant for 1980 in table 4.3, such that the greater the popu-lation density of a city, the higher the rate of homicide. This finding is consistent with the arguments of those who suggest that crowding has negative consequences for human behavior (Gove et al., 1979).

Table 4.4 shows that racial composition is the highest ranking predictor of homicide in both 1960 and 1970, with only 1970 homi-cide having a larger standardized coefficient for 1980. Female labor force participation is typically next in rank, followed by different significant effects, depending on the equation.

The finding in table 4.3 that the combination of poverty and availability has independent effects on homicide is an important one from a number of perspectives. First, it provides support for one of the major assumptions underlying the selective disinhibition approach— alcohol can enhance existing effects or, like poverty, exacerbate con-ditions already favorable to homicide. The finding has been repli-cated in an analysis at the United States state level for 1980, in which it was found that poverty by above average spirits consumption inter-action term had a significant effect on two types of homicide, robbery,

TABLE 4.4
Availability and Poverty Interaction Effects, Standardized Coefficients

Variables	1960	1970	1980
Alcohol availability	0.014	0.042	-0.017
Female labor force participation	-0.250	-0.114	-0.252
Median age	0.144	0.147	-0.021
Retail eating/drinking establishments	0.049	-0.027	0.097
Children with one parent	0.015	0.025	0.063
Social bonds composite	-0.133	0.003	-0.043
Migration	0.237	0.076	0.118
Median family income	-0.159	0.007	-0.073
Population density	0.034	0.036	0.082
Racial composition	0.489	0.619	0.339
Southern region	0.210	0.014	-0.056
One parent/availability	-0.001	0.076	-0.038
Homicide 1960		0.244	
Homicide 1970			0.467

and other felony, the latter being cases that involve a homicide and other crimes such as rape or burglary (Parker, 1992b, 1994b). Although that analysis was static in nature, it is conceivable that a dynamic analysis of types of homicide might show evidence of this interaction effect continuing into the 1980 period and beyond, for there is no reason to believe that the combination of these two homicide-inducing structural conditions has been diminished as a predictor of violence by some deliberate or accidental intervention. However, it is in terms of possible intervention that the finding of the present study is most interesting. Treatment resources will in all likelihood remain scarce over the foreseeable future, and it therefore may enhance the efficacy of such funds to target them into areas with both high availability or consumption and higher than average rates of poverty. It is in such places that treatment resources may have the most "bang" for the "buck" in terms of reducing alcohol problems and, according to the logic of this study, reducing homicide.

One possibility for the nature of the effects observed in the interaction model as well as those to be presented here is that the equations entered with the interaction terms suffer from collinearity, thus rendering the findings difficult to interpret. One of the most important ways in which collinearity could affect results such as these is by increasing the size of the standard errors. A comparison of standard errors found in tables 4.3, 4.5, and 4.7 with those found in table 4.1 puts this notion into disrepute immediately. One of the advantages of the more precise specification that the interactions terms used here provide is that their use minimizes collinearity, as only a certain, theoretically relevant part of the total distribution of each component variable is included in the interaction term.

Interaction Model #2:
Age, Availability, and City Homicide

Although a number of routine activity measures are included in this analysis, median age was selected for investigation of potential interaction effects because of its structural clarity, in terms of the theoretical approach, with regard to the expected effects. Both lifestyle theory (Hindelang et al., 1978) and routine activity (Cohen and Felson, 1979) specifically focus on young people as a locus of risk for violent crime victimization. In addition, others have asserted that age structure has a fundamental and invariant relationship with crime rates, such that the more young people a society has, the higher the crime rate of that society, regardless of history, culture, or socioeconomic conditions (Hirschi and Gottfredson, 1983). Despite the controversy this argument has engendered (Gartner and Parker, 1990; Steffensmeier and Harer, 1987), the clear expectation that a place with a younger than average population, combined with very high rates of alcohol availability, would be a place of higher rates of homicide seems a relatively straightforward extension of the routine activity and selective disinhibition approaches taken here. Tables 4.5 and 4.6 report the results of testing for such an interaction in the context of the dynamic model analyzed in this study.

   The 1960 equation contains some familiar results, including region, racial composition, female labor force participation, social bonds, migration, and median income. However, the interaction term of below average median age and higher availability has a positive, significant net effect on 1960 homicide rates. Although not as important

TABLE 4.5
Availability and Routine Activity Interaction Effects,
Metric Coefficients and Standard Errors

Variables	1960	1970	1980
Alcohol availability	-2.303[a]	1.802	-4.041
	1.283[b]	1.622	3.125
Female labor force participation	-0.231*	-0.211*	-1.069*
	0.114	0.088	0.197
Median age	0.095	0.253*	0.268*
	0.077	0.065	0.137
Retail eating/drinking establishments	0.009	0.002	0.025
	0.017	0.012	0.019
Children with one parent	0.011	-0.056	-0.088
	0.091	0.063	0.095
Social bonds composite	-0.609*	-0.065	0.224
	0.248	0.239	0.444
Migration	0.103*	0.119*	0.237*
	0.031	0.037	0.055
Median family income	-0.231*	-0.104	-0.363*
	0.114	0.092	0.143
Population density	0.022	0.045	0.222*
	0.049	0.045	0.091
Racial composition	0.199*	0.391*	0.389*
	0.036	0.035	0.058
Southern region	1.553*	-0.522	-3.413*
	0.679	0.785	1.040
Young med. age/high availability	1.628*	-1.931	-2.026
	0.828	1.819	1.449
Homicide 1960		0.318*	
		0.061	
Homicide 1970			0.530*
			0.073
Explained variance	0.510	0.652	0.649

chi-square = 1070.59   df = 365   fit index = .948
[a] = metric coefficient   [b] = standard error   * = significant effect

as the poverty/availability interaction effect for 1970 discussed previously, it is still an important piece of empirical support for the approach taken here. The fact that this interaction is not significant net of the controls for stability and change indicates that this effect may have come about as a result of a particular set of historical circumstances during the period preceding 1960. Gartner and Parker (1990), in a study that examines the invariance of age hypothesis using cross-national data, find that the proportion of young people in the United States tracks the homicide rate very well between 1920 and the late 1960s. Far from being invariant, Gartner and Parker (1990) find that this is the case only for the United States, so that findings regarding the effects of age structure like those presented in Cohen and Felson (1979) come about because of a limited focus on United States data.

Despite the interaction of age and high availability failing to reach significance in either 1970 or 1980, the more precise control for changes in the age structure that this term affords has an interesting impact on the main effect of median age in both 1970 and 1980. In both cases median age becomes a significant and positive predictor of homicide. Perhaps these findings reflect the fact that homicide has a more diverse and less concentrated age distribution than do most other types of offenses, in part because homicides occur in more diverse sets of circumstances and involve a wider range of relationships than do other crimes (Steffensmeier and Allan, 1991: 86). Thus it is the case in 1970 and 1980 that places with the higher median age had higher rates of homicide.

More precise measurement of the impact of younger average age also has an interesting effect on the estimate of the impact of the southern region in 1980, such that this effect is now negative and significant. A more complete picture is now emerging from these results, which helps to explain why the southern regional indicator has often been found to be a significant predictor of homicide. The population of southern cities is younger and poorer than those of cities in other parts of the country. Particularly under the more precise measurement of these effects that the interaction terms afford does the underlying impact of the southern region become apparent. This finding replicates one reported in Parker (1989) in which the southern regional indicator has a net negative relationship with certain types of homicide.

Table 4.6 also shows the impact of younger populations, such that when the interaction term is entered, the strength of the impact of racial composition is enhanced noticeably above that reported in table 4.2 for the main effects model. This suggests the possibility of

TABLE 4.6
Availability and Routine Activity Interaction Effects,
Standardized Coefficients

Variables	1960	1970	1980
Alcohol availability	-0.098	0.035	-0.051
Female labor force participation	-0.225	-0.090	-0.271
Median age	0.092	0.163	0.107
Retail eating/drinking establishments	0.035	0.005	0.065
Children with one parent	0.015	-0.055	-0.085
Social bonds composite	-0.159	-0.011	0.030
Migration	0.205	0.138	0.215
Median family income	-0.164	-0.060	-0.169
Population density	0.021	0.029	0.096
Racial composition	0.560	0.723	0.645
Southern region	0.171	-0.039	-0.186
Young age/high availability	0.100	-0.073	-0.055
Homicide 1960		0.201	
Homicide 1970			0.415

a further interaction between racial composition, age structure, and alcohol that is beyond the scope of the present investigation.

The overall fit of the mode presented in table 4.5 suggests that the addition of the interaction terms resulted in very little degradation in model fit; the chi-square increased less than 100 points for the extra 65 degrees of freedom, and the fit index was equal .948. Explained variance was increased in 1960, as a results of the significant interaction term, and was also noticeably higher in 1980, with the addition of several significant effects as compared to the main effects model (southern region, density, median income, median age).

Interaction Model #3:
Social Bonds, Availability and Homicide

Tables 4.7 and 4.8 present the final interaction model to be included here, in which a term combining the effects of lower than average

TABLE 4.7
Availability and Social Bonds Interaction Effects,
Metric Coefficients and Standard Errors

Variables	1960	1970	1980
Alcohol availability	-2.594[a]	-1.308	-1.471
	1.802[b]	2.155	4.290
Female labor force participation	-0.318*	-0.299*	-1.398*
	0.082	0.122	0.260
Median age	0.096	0.352	0.409*
	0.081	0.806	0.175
Retail eating/drinking establishments	0.011	0.001	0.035
	0.019	0.016	0.025
Children with one parent	0.022	-0.029	-0.113
	0.097	0.083	0.116
Social bonds composite	-0.707*	-0.034	0.115
	0.264	0.325	0.561
Migration	0.110*	0.142*	0.326*
	0.034	0.049	0.073
Median family income	-0.254*	-0.114	-0.479*
	0.123	0.124	0.188
Population density	0.024	0.063	0.283*
	0.053	0.065	0.123
Racial composition	0.196*	0.463*	0.479*
	0.037	0.043	0.069
Southern region	1.755*	-0.782	-4.681*
	0.722	1.024	1.352
Low social bond/high availability	1.911*	1.169	-4.617
	0.908	1.114	3.726
Homicide 1960		0.413*	
		0.077	
Homicide 1970			0.528*
			0.074
Explained variance	0.507	0.659	0.653

chi-square = 1168.45   df = 365   fit index = .941
[a] = metric coefficient   [b] = standard error   * = significant effect

TABLE 4.8
Availability and Social Bonds Interaction Effects,
Standardized Coefficients

Variables	1960	1970	1980
Alcohol availability	-0.120	-0.019	-0.014
Female labor force participation	-0.245	-0.097	-0.262
Median age	0.086	0.175	0.124
Retail eating/drinking establishments	0.040	0.002	0.065
Children with one parent	0.028	-0.023	-0.086
Social bonds composite	-0.176	-0.004	0.012
Migration	0.202	0.124	0.218
Median family income	-0.169	-0.049	-0.165
Population density	0.021	0.029	0.089
Racial composition	0.544	0.706	0.658
Southern region	0.184	-0.042	-0.193
Low social bond/high availability	0.102	0.033	-0.106
Homicide 1960		0.213	
Homicide 1970			0.404

social bonds, measured by a composite index of attachment to home, school, and work on the part of the city population, and high rates of alcohol availability. The overall model-fit data suggest that this model fits least well of all those discussed here, although it is similar in terms of chi-square and fit index to that presented in table 4.3. Explained variance in homicide is higher in all three equations as compared to the main effects model, especially for 1960 and 1980.

Like the age and availability interaction, the findings for 1960 support the notion that low rates of social attachments as a cause of homicide can be exacerbated in the presence of very high rates of availability. Racial composition, region, female labor force participation, migration, median income, and the main effect of social bonds are also significant predictors of 1960 homicide rates. For 1970 the results show that female labor force, migration, racial composition, and 1960 homicide are significant, and for 1980, the results are very nearly the same as those in table 4.5, with both region and median age having significant, counter-expectation effects, and median income and density have significant consistent effects.

Table 4.8 once again shows the dominance in terms of racial composition, 1960 and 1970 homicide, and female labor force participation, followed by migration. These four variables have the most consistent strength and significance across the four models presented and the three time periods considered. Overall, these results provide support for the routine activity approach and the social bonds approach, with support for the economic deprivation approach coming only indirectly, in terms of a significant interaction effect, and in terms of the negative impact of median income in some of the interaction models. In addition, the southern regional hypothesis has taken a major hit in terms of this dynamic model, as compared to other recent analyses that have found support for continuity using static models for the same general time periods analyzed here.

Stability Effects: Homicide, Availability, and Other Factors

The discussion so far has concentrated on the impact of change, rather than on the stability of the variables included in the model. The one exception to that is for homicide, although the precise nature of the stability results for homicide has not been explicitly presented. Table 4.9 presents average stability effects, in terms of standardized coefficients, for all the measures included in the analyses discussed here.

In general the stability estimates for the independent variables used in these models are relatively high, ranging from a low of .648 for the impact of children living with one parent in 1970 on the same measure in 1980, to a high of .999 for median age between 1970 and 1980. The stability estimates for homicide, on the other hand, are relatively low, in part because there was a great deal of change during this time period in homicide rates, but also because homicide is the dependent variable in the equations estimated here. As a result some of the other predictors help to explain a substantial part of the change from decade to decade in homicide rates, thus leaving the prior homicide rate to account for the change that is unaccounted for by other factors. The stability estimates for the other variables in the model would also be reduced if equations were

TABLE 4.9
Average Stability Coefficients, Main Effects,
and Three Interaction Models, Average Standardized Coefficients

Variables	1960-1970	1970-1980
Alcohol availability	0.679	0.857
Female labor force participation	0.896	0.890
Median age	0.928	0.999
Retail eating/drinking establishments	0.735	0.968
Children with one parent	0.882	0.648
Social bonds composite	0.782	0.809
Migration	0.876	0.921
Median family income	0.941	0.917
Population density	0.946	0.972
Racial composition	0.942	0.978
Homicide 1960	0.224	
Homicide 1970		0.440
Poverty/availability interaction	0.610	0.616
Young age/availability interaction	0.555	0.480
Social bonds/avail. interaction	0.367	0.546

developed to explain them as dependent variables. As for the interaction terms, these show less stability than the remaining independent variables, but more than the homicide rates. The explanation for this lies in the fact that these terms were appropriately calculated separately for each decade, which means that the same cities included in 1960 may not have been included in 1970 or 1980, thus decreasing the stability estimate.

What can these stability coefficients tell us? The very fact that the homicide stability estimates are so low indicates that, at least in part, the model proposed here to explain homicide has been successful. Second, the moderate stability of the interaction terms suggests that these terms are sensitive to the changes occurring in the joint distribution of alcohol availability and the three variables used to measure the interactions. Third, the relatively high stability estimates found for most of the independent variables demonstrates the importance of the modeling approach used here. Both stability and change in the effects of these variables on homicide is inappropriately estimated when the stability in these measures is not accounted for.

Summary

The results of these four tests of the implications at the macrolevel of the selective disinhibition approach provide reasonable empirical support for the notion that alcohol plays a significant role in the generation of homicide. An independent net effect of alcohol availability on homicide rates was found in the equation for 1970, even with the stability of homicide and the other measures in the model controlled for. In addition, the accompanying idea that the impact of alcohol in general is to enhance the effects of factors that are thought to cause homicide was also supported in terms of the finding that the combined effects of high rates of poverty and availability were found to have an independent net effect on homicide, again in the 1970 equation, once again with the stability of homicide and the other independent variables controlled. These results show that between 1960 and 1980 in the United States alcohol contributed in an important way to the increase in homicide rates experienced by the country as a whole and the 256 cities examined here. Finally, the results for the interaction terms involving social bonds and younger age structures further illustrate the role that alcohol plays in causing homicide.

Considering these results with regard to the standard models of homicide used in the criminological research literature, the results concerning alcohol gain in importance. Although some traditionally strong and consistent findings from that body of research are replicated, such as the impact of racial composition on homicide, some of the most important findings in that body of research are specifically undermined. The contrast between recent results concerning supposedly stable impact of the southern region on homicide (Land et al., 1990) and those reported in this chapter, in which the southern regional indicator shows little stability and consistency in a model that accounts appropriately for stability and change in homicide, are telling. The approach taken here to empirically examining the role of alcohol in homicide has been demanding, and alcohol availability, as compared with some of the most enduring findings in the field, has faired very well.

These relatively positive results in a basic test of the impact of alcohol on homicide set the stage for addressing the question of policy designed to break the alcohol and violence link. If alcohol does play in role in homicide, can policies designed to reduce alcohol consumption and availability reduce homicide? The results reported and discussed in chapter 5, in which the net impact of increasing the legal minimum age of purchase on youth-specific homicide is examined, will provide an answer to these questions. The results reported here make such questions a legitimate topic for further research.

Chapter 5

Alcohol Policy and Crime Control

This chapter presents the results from a study of the impact on youth homicide victimization of the greatest social experiment of the 1980s, the nationwide increase in the legal minimum age of purchase for alcoholic beverages. The design and measurement of variables to be included in this analysis were described in chapter 3. However, it will be useful in interpreting these results if, before providing them here, discussion of the background of this study is presented. First, a discussion of the recent history of minimum age of purchase laws in the United States is presented, followed by a review of the literature in which the impact of such laws on youth drinking, youth drinking and driving, and youth fatalities in drinking and driving crashes is outlined. A brief discussion of the history and logic of the design and method used to estimate the results is presented next, with the presentation and discussion of the results concluding this chapter.

RECENT HISTORY OF MINIMUM AGE LAWS:
TWO GREAT SOCIAL EXPERIMENTS

The recent history of changes in minimum age laws represents one of the most interesting cases of policy change and the use of research to evaluate such change. One of the interesting aspects of this example is that minimum age of purchase was first decreased and then later increased, providing an unusual example of a fully specified quasi-experimental design (Campbell and Stanley, 1963; Cook and Campbell, 1979). In most examples that come to mind, a policy change is put into place. The task of the evaluator is to distinguish the effect of the policy change on some outcome, independent of all the other changes that are occurring simultaneously as the time from the policy change accumulates. In the case of minimum age laws, however, twenty-nine United States states first lowered the minimum age of purchase for alcohol during the period 1970 to 1975 (Wagenaar, 1983: 3). During the period between 1976 through 1988, all of these states, and all other states that had minimum ages of less than 21, raised the minimum age of purchase to 21. It is extremely rare for policy changes to occur at such a breakneck speed, at least for government entities like state governments. What was going on that caused all this change and counterchange to occur?

In the case of the earlier period of the lowering of minimum age laws, this phenomenon must be placed into the context of the late 1960s and early 1970s. During this period a number of aspects of the public policy arena combined to focus attention on youth, and the position of youth, legally and socially, in United States society. The increasing unpopularity of the Vietnam war, and the mounting public protests against this conflict, focused attention on the participation of youth both as soldiers in the war and as protesters at home. This focus spilled over into a general consideration of the legal status of young people in the United States, an effort that revealed some major discrepancies in the ability of young people to actively participate in society. Although many males aged 18 to 20 were participating in the Vietnam war as combatants, they and their same-age companions were denied the right to vote in the United States until reaching the age of 21. Similarly, a number of other barriers to the full participation of young people in the legal and social aspects of society—marriage without parental consent, legal access to contraceptive devices, the ability to enter into legally binding contracts, being eligible for jury duty, and so on—had all been extended to those who had reached the age of 18 during the 1960s. In 1970 the U.S. Congress extended the right to vote in federal elections to individuals aged 18 and older, having reduced the minimum qualifying age from 21 (Wagenaar, 1983: 2). During the early 1970s, then, the pressure on minimum age of purchase laws intensified, as these laws became almost that last of the rites of passage separating youth from adults. It was in this context that a majority of states lowered the minimum age of purchase to 18 years in most cases, and applied this new lower minimum to any legal alcoholic beverage, again in most cases (Wagenaar, 1983: table 1-1).

In the wake of this movement toward lower minimum age of purchase, a number of studies appeared that were designed to evaluate the impact of this change on availability to and consumption of alcohol to young people. These studies focused primarily on alcohol-related automobile crashes as an outcome most likely to be effected by the policy change. One of the reasons for this focus was that highway crash statistics show that young males in particular are overrepresented in highway crashes, both fatal and nonfatal. For example, Carsten (1981) reports that the fatality rate for young males and for young females is six times and three times, respectively, the rate of fatalities for older drivers. Although crashes involving alcohol are a smaller proportion of the total than is the case with older drivers, the fact that young drivers have such high rates of crashes in general means that young drivers are at greater risk of an injury or fatality in a drinking- and driving-related accident (Waller et al., 1970; Ferris et al., 1976).

A number of studies that specifically examined the impact of lower minimum age laws concluded that alcohol-related fatalities and crashes increased significantly in Massachusetts (Cucchiaro et al., 1974), Maine and Michigan (Douglas et al., 1974), Ontario, Canada (Whitehead et al., 1975), and for the United States as a whole (Cook and Tauchen, 1982, 1984). As additional evidence accumulated to suggest that decreasing the minimum age of purchase was having a negative impact on alcohol-related crashes (Males, 1986; Vingilis and DeGenova, 1984), and a grassroots antidrunk driving movement began to gain strength (groups like MADD and SADD), a number of states had begun to reverse the trend of the early 1970s. Minnesota, which had lowered the minimum age for the purchase of all alcoholic beverages from 21 to 18 years in June 1973, was the first state to reverse the trend, increasing the minimum age of purchase for all beverages to 19 in September 1976 (Wagenaar, 1983: 3-4). The public pressure and accumulating evidence resulted in the passage of federal legislation, effective in 1984, that encouraged all states to pass an increase in the minimum age of purchase for all alcoholic beverages by 1986, or risk losing a significant portion of one of the few remaining important revenue-sharing programs (in which the federal government returns revenues it collects to the states)—the highway trust fund (O'Malley and Wagenaar, 1991). As this is a major source of funding that states depend on for highway construction and repair, this negative incentive was significant enough to result in the passage of a uniform minimum age of purchase of 21 years in all states by 1988 (Distilled Spirits Council, 1989).

Since the beginning of the trend towards increasing the minimum age of purchase, a number of additional studies have demonstrated that the earlier finding of a decrease in minimum age resulting in an increase in crashes and fatalities among youth was no fluke. The new research shows quite clearly that increasing the minimum age of purchase resulted in a significant decrease in traffic fatalities among youth. O'Malley and Wagenaar (1991) also show that self-reports by youth of alcohol consumption decreased significantly after the implementation of the higher minimum age of purchase. Saffer and Grossman (1987), in a design similar to that used here, show that the higher minimum age of purchase had an independent and negative effect on motor vehicle death rates of those 18-20 years of age, controlling for a number of important factors including beer tax rates and a measure of alcohol availability.

The recent history of change and evaluation, and again change and evaluation, of a major policy initiative, occurring nationwide and affecting millions of young people that the example of the minimum age of purchase for alcohol portrays, is unprecedented in the history of applied social research. This is a textbook example of how the power of an experimental design can be approached by what are, from the point of view of the analyst, naturally occurring events. Cook and Campbell (1979: 225) refer to this design as the quasi experiment. They suggest that it can be a very strong design in terms of the ability of the researcher employing this design to rule out potential threats to validity. However, the question of interest in the present analysis, whether this intervention had any impact on youth homicide, seems quite removed from the results of studies that assess the impact of increasing the minimum age of purchase on youthful drunk driving and associated negative outcomes. There is no evidence that has been discovered to suggest that legislators, political leaders, researchers, or grassroots lobbyists had any notion that this legal change would have an effect on youth homicide rates. Why is the question of the impact of minimum age of purchase for alcohol on youth homicide rates legitimate to ask?

First, the notion that there may be such an effect is consistent with the process of selective disinhibition that underlies this entire study. If, under some circumstances, disputes involving youth under the influence of alcohol sometimes lead to violence and homicide, as described in chapter 2, then any intervention that reduces availability and consumption of alcohol by young people (as has been conclusively demonstrated for this particular intervention [O'Malley and Wagenaar, 1991]), may in fact reduce youth homicide victimization. In addition, the analyses in chapter 4 demonstrate that the implications of selective disinhibition concerning the relationship of availability and violence have some merit, such that it is reasonable to ask if a specific availability reduction might have an effect on a specific type of violence involving as victims the individuals whose availability is being restricted by raising the minimum age of purchase for alcohol. Finally, it has been suggested that policies designed to indirectly restrict the availability of alcoholic beverages, such as taxes on such beverages, have a similar impact on violent crime in general as that hypothesized here concerning the impact of minimum age of purchase on homicide (Cook and Moore, 1993a). If the indirect restriction of alcohol availability, through the mechanism of increased prices due to increased taxation, is found to have an impact on violence in general, it also seems reasonable to expect that a direct and specific limitation on availability would have a measurable impact on a specific type of violent crime.

The precision of this analysis is further enhanced by the fact that a specific prediction can be made for particular types of youth homicide, as was previously described in chapter 3. It is no coincidence that the time period selected for consideration of the effect of minimum age of purchase, 1976 through 1983, a time period just prior to the passage of the previously described federal incentive, and a time period in which nineteen states implemented increases in the minimum age of purchase, is also a time period for which very good and detailed youth homicide data are available (Federal Bureau of Investigation, 1987).

As explained previously, these data allow for the classification of homicide into two categories: primary and nonprimary (Parker and Smith, 1979; Radelet, 1981). *Primary* homicide occurs when the victim and the offender knew each other prior to the event of homicide. This category includes people who are family members, spouses, boy friends and girl friends, lovers, friends, and acquaintances. *Nonprimary* homicide includes those that occur between victims and offenders for whom these is no known prior primary relationship. Such crimes often take place in the context of other serious crimes like robbery, burglary, or sexual assault. Considering the selective disinhibition argument, and the process whereby active constraint can sometimes be overcome when alcohol is present in either victim or offender, the most logical prediction to make is that increases in the minimum age of purchase for alcohol are most likely to have an impact on primary homicides. Primary homicides fit well with the conceptualization of interpersonal disputes that forms the basis of the argument linking homicide and alcohol adopted here.

Estimation and Design: Minimum Age
of Purchase and Youth Homicide

To refresh the reader concerning the summary of the research design for this analysis, the most appropriate way to evaluate this quasi experiment is to use an approach that pools the cross-sectional position of each state in the United States with the overtime trends of homicide, changes in the minimum age of purchase, and the remaining variables. In essence this provides us with a set of multiple replications, makes it easy to deal with the fact that the intervention happens at different time points in each state, and allows for the introduction of control variables that could account for any observed relationship between minimum purchase age and the two types of youth homicide to be included. This pooling of cross-sectional and time-serial data creates some inherent problems for statistical estimation. These are problems that have been thoroughly investigated in the literature and for which standard solutions exist, which have been utilized here (Saffer and Grossman, 1987; Gartner, 1990; Stimson, 1985; Nerlove, 1971; Maddala, 1971). Technical details of the estimation, the diagnosis of these problems, and their correction in the final estimates are discussed in Appendix 1; descriptive data on the measured used in this analysis are given in Appendix 2C.

The independent variable of major interest, the intervention of increasing the minimum age of purchase for alcoholic beverages, was taken from O'Malley and Wagenaar (1991: 481), and took the form of a dummy variable: a score of 1 indicated that in a particular year and state, the intervention had taken place—that is, the minimum age had been increased at least one year—and a score of 0 otherwise. As indicated in table 1 of O'Malley and Wagenaar (1991:481), some states increased the minimum age of purchase gradually over several years, while others raised it from 18 to 21 in one year. The intervention measured used here does not distinguish these two paths to the intervention. The intervention measure retains the value of 1 once the minimum age of purchase has been changed until the end of the current observation period, 1983. If the change is effective on a date other than January 1 of the given year, the intervention is assigned to the *current* year if the law took effect on or before July 1, and to the *following* year if the change took place after that date. In the period under consideration here, 1976-83, a total of nineteen states implemented an increase in the minimum age of purchase, the first taking effect (as measured here) in 1977 for the state of Minnesota and the last for the states of New York, Ohio, and West Virginia in 1983 (O'Malley and Wagenaar, 1991: 481).

As described in chapter 3, additional variables in the model include economic inequality, infant mortality (a measure of poverty; Loftin and Hill, 1974; Loftin and Parker, 1985), beer consumption, proportion of the population that is nonwhite, the total population, and the southern regional indicator. The units of analysis are the fifty-one United States states (including the District of Columbia), and the time period analyzed is 1976 to 1983, yielding 408 observations (51 by 8).

As compared to the list of variables used in the analysis of city availability in chapter 4, there is significant overlap in the inclusion of racial composition, the most important and consistent predictor of city homicide rates, as well as with the inclusion of a poverty measure and the regional southern indicator. Given that the unit of analysis is the state, direct measures of consumption are available, and should be included for the reasons discussed in chapter 3, but the choice of beer consumption is justified on a number of grounds. First, beer is the dominant alcoholic beverage consumed in the United States, accounting for more than half of all alcohol consumed (Williams et al., 1992; Treno and Parker, 1993). As was reported in chapter 1, the United States ranks seventh overall in beer consumption compared to other industrialized countries. In addition, it seems clear from studies of youth consumption and youth drunk driving that beer is the beverage of choice among young people: Treno and Parker (1993) find that a measure of the age structure that focuses on those aged 20 to 29 is significantly related to beer consumption between 1950 and 1986. Saffer and Grossman (1987) find that beer taxes have a significant net impact on single vehicle nighttime crashes among young drivers (the most frequently used proxy for alcohol-related crashes). As Cook and Moore (1993a: 154) point out, young drinkers prefer beer, and the young are disproportionately involved in violence, so it is logical to select beer consumption as the appropriate measure. In the current study this logic is strengthened by the fact that youth homicide is the dependent variable, so that there is a direct logical connection between the choice of alcohol indicator and the dependent variables.

Two other variables are included in this analysis as controls— inequality and total population. The former has had a long history in the homicide research literature, although the results have been contradictory as to the impact of inequality on homicide (Blau and Blau, 1982; Williams, 1984; Crutchfield, 1989). Total population has been used here, as well as in a number of other studies (Loftin and Parker, 1985; Sampson, 1985; Bailey, 1984; Land et al., 1990), as a proxy for a number of unmeasured variables.

The two types of homicide are analyzed in three age categories: 15 to 18, 19 to 20, and 21 to 24. The logic of these age categories, as described in greater detail in chapter 3, is that those aged 15-18 may have reduced homicide after the intervention because it is now much harder for them to obtain alcohol. A lower minimum age of purchase would in most cases allow 18-year-olds to buy alcohol not only for themselves but also for their friends who are 15 to 17 years of age. The 19- and 20-year-olds should be most directly affected. These individuals had legal access under the previous lower minimum age of purchase, but they are now specifically excluded. Those aged 21 to 24 are included to examine the impact of the legal change on those just at or just above the limit. Evidence from longitudinal studies of college drinking suggests that individuals who reach 21 under a 21-year-old minimum purchase law will have a different, and more moderate, history of alcohol consumption than those who start using alcohol earlier (Saltz and Elandt, 1986).

Results: Minimum Age of Purchase, Beer Consumption, and Type of Youth Homicide

Table 5.1 presents these results, with the unstandardized coefficient, the standard error, and the value of the t statistic (coefficient divided by standard error) given, respectively, for each independent variable; starred coefficients are those that reached statistical significance.

Results presented in table 5.1 suggest that increases in the minimum age of purchase for alcohol may have indeed had some impact on youth homicide. One of the six coefficients for minimum age of purchase is significant and negative, so that increases in the minimum age reduced homicide victimizations among those aged 21 to 24 during the period 1976 through 1983. This finding is first of all consistent with the prediction, based on the selective disinhibition approach, that primary youth homicide, rather than nonprimary youth homicide, would be the most likely to be affected by this legal change. In addition, the fact that the effect is found for those just over the ages directly affected by the change supports research on the impact of early versus late onset drinking, in which later onset leads to a different, and more moderate, drinking history, which in turn should be related to lower rates of alcohol-related problems, including violence (Saltz and Elandt, 1986; O'Malley and Wagenaar, 1991: 484).

Further evidence in support of the notion that minimum age of purchase increases had some effect on youth homicides can be seen in the overall pattern of the results reported here. For example, although all six coefficients for minimum age are negative (a kind of face validity measure of the underlying notion), the three coefficients for primary homicide are substantially larger and the two insignificant coefficients are much closer to statistical significance than are any of the three effect estimates for nonprimary homicide. Although caution should be used in the interpretation of nonsignificant results, this consistent pattern across the estimates, and the differences by type of homicide, are additional findings that can be taken as supporting the prediction that minimum drinking age increases had some preventive effect on youth homicide during this period of time.

A second interesting set of results that are relevant for this study in table 5.1 are those for the effect of beer consumption on youth homicide. In five of the six equations, that for primary homicide victims aged 21 to 24 being the exception, beer consumption has a significant and positive effect on youth homicide. These findings not only replicate research on alcohol-related traffic deaths (Saffer and Grossman, 1987; Gruenewald and Ponicki, 1993), but also research on the impact of beer taxation (and by implication, consumption) on homicide in general for the period 1979 through 1988, a time frame that overlaps that used here substantially (Cook and Moore, 1993a). These findings clearly suggest that there is more than can be done to reduce youth homicide in the way of alcohol-related policies. It is clear also from the estimates presented in table 5.1 that any significant reduction in beer consumption would result in a significant decrease in youth homicide.

As was the case for the findings for availability in 1970, homicide, and spirits consumption in the aggregate, the validity of the finding here that beer consumption has a major impact on youth homicide is consistent with national trends during the 1976 to 1983 time period in aggregate beer consumption. Figure 5.1, which shows beer consumption in gallons of pure alcohol equivalent, show that

FIGURE 5.1
Beer Consumption, 1950-86

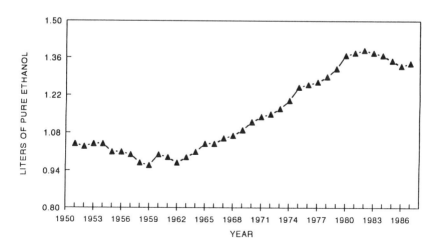

TABLE 5.1
Minimum Age of Purchase and Youth Homicide

Independent Variable	Primary Homicide 15-18	Primary Homicide 19-20	Primary Homicide 21-24	Nonprimary Homicide 15-18	Nonprimary Homicide 19-20	Nonprimary Homicide 21-24
Inequality	0.0016	-0.0044	0.0023	-0.0008	-0.0005	-0.0001
	(0.0019)	(0.0030)	(0.0400)	(0.0024)	(0.0004)	(0.0003)
	0.8421	-1.4758	0.0575	-0.3227	1.2500	-0.3333
Infant mortality	0.0012	0.0031	0.0003	0.0023	0.0025	0.0039
	(0.0005)	(0.0010)	(0.0010)	(0.0006)	(0.0011)	(0.0010)
	2.4000**	3.1042**	0.3000	3.8333**	2.3104**	3.9670**
Beer consumption	0.2171	0.1072	0.0321	0.1573	0.1045	0.3137
	(0.0701)	(0.0635)	(0.0454)	(0.0731)	(0.0245)	(0.0433)
	3.0970**	1.6882**	0.7118	2.1518**	4.2653**	7.2448**
Minimum age changes	-0.0029	-0.0069	-0.0084	-0.0016	-0.0014	-0.0021
	(0.0024)	(0.0051)	(0.0052)	(0.0030)	(0.0049)	(0.0044)
	-1.2029	-1.3578	-1.6231**	-0.5453	-0.2927	-0.4699

(continued on next page)

TABLE 5.1 (continued)

Independent Variable	Primary Homicide 15-18	Primary Homicide 19-20	Primary Homicide 21-24	Nonprimary Homicide 15-18	Nonprimary Homicide 19-20	Nonprimary Homicide 21-24
Proportion nonwhite	0.0164 (0.0096) 1.7032**	0.0303 (0.2020) 1.4984	0.0670 (0.0233) 2.8752**	0.0510 (0.0157) 3.2471**	0.1525 (0.0328) 4.6435**	0.1466 (0.0323) 4.5358**
Southern region	0.0108 (0.0030) 3.6173**	0.0339 (0.0063) 5.3993**	0.0411 (0.0074) 5.5373**	-0.0020 (0.0047) -0.4331	0.0066 (0.0098) 0.6728	0.0186 (0.0097) 1.9242**
Total population	0.0010 (0.00029) 3.4482**	0.0008 (0.0003) 2.6667**	0.0007 (0.0003) 2.3333**	0.0023 (0.0004) 5.7500**	0.0029 (0.0005) 5.8000**	0.0031 (0.0006) 5.1667**
Explained variance (OLS)	0.346	0.374	0.488	0.416	0.510	0.579
Rho	0.281 (AR 1)	0.272 (AR 1)	0.505 (AR 1)	0.250 (E.C.)	0.429 (E.C.)	0.500 (E.C.)

** significant with probability at .05 or less, one-tailed test

beer consumption was steadily increasing during the 1970s and into the early 1980s. In 1983, the final year in the data analyzed here, beer consumption had eased off its peak in 1981 of 1.39 gallons of pure alcohol equivalent to 1.37 gallons per capita, so that the impact of the steady increase in beer consumption was still evident through the end of the period examined here.

Findings reported in table 5.1 for poverty replicate a number of studies that show this to be an important predictor of homicide rates (Parker and Toth, 1990; Parker, 1989; Williams, 1984; Bailey, 1984). As was the case with beer consumption, the only equation in which this coefficient does not reach significance was that for primary homicide victims aged 21 to 24. This replicates the pattern of findings reported by Parker and Toth (1990), in which this same measure of poverty—infant mortality—had a significant impact on total homicide and on three of four types of homicide, with the exception being for primary intimate, a category that includes lovers, boyfriends/girlfriends, and other nonmarital but sexually intimate relationships. These latter types of homicide are likely to be a substantial portion of those included in homicides analyzed here for 21 to 24 year olds.

The effects of racial composition given in table 5.1, like those discussed in chapter 4, show that this variable is an important predictor of youth homicide as well. Five of the six types are positively predicted by racial composition net of the other variables in the model. The exception to this pattern is in the equation for primary homicide victims aged 19 and 20, in which racial composition adds no net predictive power to the model. This finding is also consistent with results reported in Parker (1989), in which racial composition failed to predict a type of homicide that is likely to be a substantial portion of those in the primary 19- and 20-year-old rate analyzed here, that being family intimate—spouses and ex-spouses.

The impact of the southern region reported in table 5.1 is interesting, given the results discussed in chapter 4 with regard to this indicator. As the reader will recall, these previously discussed results showed that the impact of the southern regional indicator went from positive and significant in 1960, to insignificant in 1970, and finally to significant and negative in 1980. The results presented in table 5.1 provide part of the explanation for such findings, as it will be recalled from the discussion in chapter 2 that the trends during the last thirty years with regard to homicide by type of victim offender relationship are that primary categories have declined and nonprimary categories have increased as a proportion of the total. In the findings presented in table 5.1, the southern regional indicator is a clear and consistent net predictor of primary homicide, but it is a mixed predictor at best for nonprimary homicide. The negative finding for 1980 presented in chapter 4 for overall homicide could in fact be masking two, divergent effects, one positive for primary and family homicide rates, and the other negative, for nonprimary types. These findings are consistent with two other studies in which the impact of the southern regional indicator varied depending on the type of homicide analyzed. Parker (1989) found that other felony homicide, a category of nonprimary homicides that occur during crimes other than robberies (burglaries, rapes, auto thefts), was negatively associated with the southern region. Parker and Toth (1990) found that the southern regional indicator was significantly related to family and other primary intimate homicides, but not to nonfamily and other nonintimate homicides. These findings, along with both sets of findings presented here and in chapter 4, suggest that the impact of the southern region on homicide is concentrated on those involving close, often sexually intimate, family relationships. The entire history of the impact of the southern region on homicide may be explained by the fact that when such research was undertaken in quantitative studies, in the mid to late 1960s, these types of homicide were a large portion of the national total, and perhaps a particularly large portion of homicide committed in the south. However, as the southern region, as well as the rest of the country, moved to a situation in which family intimate homicides became a smaller and smaller portion of the total, the impact of the southern region became less pronounced on homicides as a whole, and in fact was negatively related to nonfamily intimate types of homicide that were not only growing in the southern region, but in the rest of the country as well.

The total population's effects on youth homicide are strong and consistent, but in this case the conclusion holds for all six types of homicide. Clearly there are a number of omitted variables for which this indicator is serving as a proxy here. A list of the members of this omitted variable list will be discussed in chapter 6 in some detail.

Finally, the results for inequality in table 5.1 show that this variable is insignificant in all six equations estimated. Perhaps this is a reflection of the fact that the measure used here, which is based on the difference in concentration at the upper and lower tails of the distribution, fails to capture important variation in inequality that may be related to youth homicide. It may also be the case that these findings replicate a number of studies that have examined a wide variety of inequality measures, and which find that it has little or no impact on homicide net of other factors (Parker and Toth, 1990; Williams, 1984).

SUMMARY

The findings on the question of whether a policy designed to control alcohol availability and, by implication, alcohol consumption of young people might also have an impact on youth homicide were presented and discussed here. Some modest evidence was presented that the increases in the minimum age of purchase for alcoholic beverages had a negative impact on youth homicides, particularly those primary homicides in which the victim and the offender knew each other before the homicide occurred. Further evidence on the potential efficacy of alcohol control measures in the effort to control homicide was also presented in the form of the strong, consistent, and positive effects that beer consumption was found to have on both primary and nonprimary youth homicide. In addition, these findings were estimated in the context of a model that controlled for the impact of some of the major causes of homicide in the research literature, including poverty, racial composition, the southern region, and total population size. These results demonstrate the potential of policies designed to control alcohol availability and consumption for preventing homicide and other forms of violence.

Both sets of analyses presented here provide support for the basic theoretical model identified in this study, selective disinhibition, that links alcohol to homicide, and both studies are indicative of the ways in which alcohol-related public policies may be utilized to address the problem of escalating rates of violence in the United States. Both studies raise a number of interesting questions, both in terms of the findings and their interpretation, and by the unaddressed yet potentially very relevant questions in each analysis. In chapter 6 this study will conclude by examining these questions in terms of a multiyear and multiproject research program that is designed to extend knowledge of the alcohol and violence link, further investigate policy changes related to alcohol that can affect violence, and provide answers to some of the unanswered and unaddressed questions raised by the efforts reported and described in the present study.

Chapter 6

SOME UNANSWERED QUESTIONS ABOUT ALCOHOL AND HOMICIDE

This project has been designed to address what has clearly been an underresearched topic in both criminology and in alcohol research—the link between alcohol and homicide. Historical and international comparative arguments and data have been presented to suggest that the strength and significance of this link is reasonably unique to the United States, at least in comparison to other industrialized, developed, mostly northern hemisphere nations of North America, Europe, and Asia. Theoretical arguments have been marshaled to describe how alcohol could be related to homicide, with some attention to the problem of why only a relatively few cases of interpersonal disputes that are alcohol-involved result in homicide. The implications of this theoretical argument have been traced to the macrosocial level, where an appropriate set of research questions about variation in alcohol and homicide can be framed and appropriately addressed with reasonably good data. Two empirical analyses have been described, estimated, presented, and discussed—analyses that were designed to address the question of the relationship between alcohol and homicide, and further, how public policy might be able to address this relationship and prevent some alcohol-related violence from occurring.

In the end, a reasonable case, supported by historical, theoretical, and empirical evidence, has been made that alcohol and violence are causally linked, and that alcohol control policy has some efficacy in any attempt to control and prevent violence. None of the evidence presented here is strongly compelling, none of it overwhelms all opposition so as to completely convince the reader of the validity of these conclusions, but taken as a whole, a consistent, clear, and reasonable case is made by what has been presented here that alcohol and homicide are linked in some very important ways.

However, as is the case in any research project, a number of questions remain unanswered or unaddressed by all that has been presented previously. It is customary at this point in a book like this to discuss what future research ought to address if some of the problems and weaknesses of the current project are to be overcome. It often seems as if these discussions have little influence on the course of research in the substantive area of the book, either on the part of those reading the book or on the part of the author. Sometimes it is very clear that what is needed to address the problems in the present research is conceivable but impractical, sometimes even impossible to achieve. What will be offered here, in contrast, is a description of four research projects that are either already underway, about to be funded, or in proposal development stage, all of which address what can be seen as important shortcomings in the present research, and all of which either are being done, will be done, or for which a serious attempt to secure funding to complete them is in progress.

It is, of course, the case that even when and if these future projects are completed, the questions they have addressed will still need further answers, or better answers, than these projects can provide. Further, these projects address only a small number of what may be a large number of important unaddressed and unanswered questions raised by the present research; no attempt to delineate this territory of shortcomings, weaknesses, unaddressed and unanswered questions will be made here beyond the four projects to be described below (the critics must be allowed some room to perform their functions with distinction). Others may also view the priorities placed here upon certain kinds of questions to be wrong or misguided. No claims are made that the issues addressed in the four research projects are clearly the next ones that should be addressed, or that these projects address the most pressing or most important of the remaining issues. The only stipulation to be offered concerning these projects, the issues they raise, and the way these projects address the current research, is that they are interesting to both the author and to sources of research funding.

UNADDRESSED ISSUES CONCERNING MINIMUM AGE OF PURCHASE LAWS AND YOUTH HOMICIDE

Perhaps the most important unaddressed issue in the analysis presented in chapter 5 has to do with the time frame included in the analysis. Designs like this always benefit from additional base line time—that is, time before the intervention occurs—and postintervention time—that is, time after the interventions have been implemented so that their lasting effects, if any, can be ascertained. By the end of 1983, most states had yet to pass increases in the minimum age of purchase. The lack of postintervention time may cut both ways, however, and this is a likely explanation for the absence of effects in table 5.1 for two of three types of primary homicide, and perhaps even for the nonprimary types. If the data were extended to 1991, for example, all states had passed this intervention and had at least four full postintervention years over which to gauge the impact of the intervention. In the analysis presented in chapter 5, some of the impact of the minimum age of purchase could be undermined by cross-border effects, in which young people in a state that has increased the minimum age of purchase visit a nearby state that has not-for alcohol purchases. However, by 1988 all the states had increased the minimum age, eliminating the possibility of border effects (Saffer and Grossman, 1987:412; O'Malley and Wagenaar, 1991).

A second set of issues, which pertain to the availability analysis as well as to the minimum age of purchase analysis, involves the impact of race/ethnicity and gender on the causal relationships among alcohol, minimum age of purchase, and homicide. Just as it became clear some years ago that analyzing primary and nonprimary homicide separately would lead to major differences in the empirical evaluation of theories and hypotheses about the causes of homicide, it has become increasingly clear that the analysis of race, ethnicity, and gender-specific homicide rates will lead to important differences in the evaluation of similar theories and hypotheses.

Although racial composition was included in this analysis, as Messner and Sampson (1991) and Huff-Corzine, Corzine, and Moore (1991) have demonstrated, many of the predictors of homicide operate differentially on race-specific homicide rates. In other words, the fact that proportion nonwhite has a significant t-value in five of the six equations estimated here cannot be taken as indicative of an additive effect for racial composition on homicide. Recent research has shown conclusively that this apparently additive effect masks a number of significant interactions. For example, Sampson (1987) finds that two economic deprivation measures—percent of children living in female-headed households, and average welfare payment—have greater impact on African-American youth robbery rates than on non African-American rates. An examination of race-specific rates of homicide may reveal that among African-Americans poverty has such a strong impact that any additional impact of the minimum age of purchase intervention is insignificant, while the opposite may be true for non African-Americans.

Recent research has also shown that the factors that predict male homicide victimization are not completely identical to those that predict female victimization (Browne and Williams, 1989; Gartner, 1990; Parker, 1992b). An examination of both race/ethnic and gender-specific victimization rates could be essential in delimiting the precise nature of any impact of increases in the minimum age of purchase. For example, it may be the case that the intervention has its greatest impact on female victimization rates, as women are most often killed by men in the context of a primary style victim/offender relationship. If, as shown in chapter 5, decreased access via increased minimum age of purchase has its greatest impact on primary homicides, a gender-based interaction of this type would be the appropriate way to test for this kind of relationship.

Another set of considerations involves the way in which age was categorized. Although an argument can be made (and was made in chapters 3 and 5) about the utility of including 18-year-olds with those 15 to 17, this categorization may downwardly bias the estimated effect of minimum age of purchase on youth homicide. In addition, the statistical power of the analysis in chapter 5 may be too low to detect small but substantively important effects of the minimum age of purchase. Extending the data both backward into the base line period, and forward into the postintervention period, for example, including data for 1973 to 1990 or 1991, would enable the model to detect even small effects—that is, effects that add only 2 percent at the .05 probability level, to the explained variance of homicide, assuming twelve other variables in the model, with power exceeded .99 (Cohen, 1977: 407-53).

Perhaps most importantly, though, is the fact that the analysis presented here may be misspecified, leading again to a downward bias in the estimated effects of minimum age of purchase on homicide. In order to gauge the impact of minimum age of purchase on consumption, other influences on aggregate consumption would have to be included as well, so as to appropriately ascertain the independent effect of raising the minimum age of purchase on alcohol consumption. In each of the ways discussed in chapters 3 and 5 that minimum age of purchase and youth homicide are linked, it is through consumption that these relationships operate. However, it is

FIGURE 6.1
Minimum Age, Alcohol, and Homicide

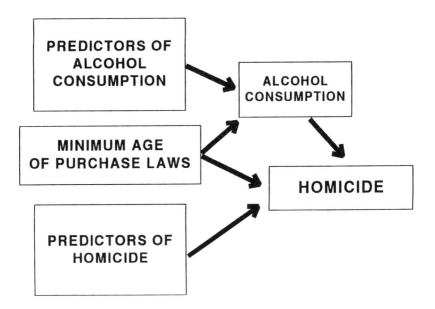

also conceivable that minimum age of purchase would have a direct effect on youth homicide rates independent of an indirect effect through consumption. If the impact of raising the minimum age of purchase on aggregate consumption is minimal—either because nonyouth consumption accounts for the vast majority of total consumption, or because increases in consumption by those who do become eligible to drink legally makes up for the lack of consumption by younger persons, or because lax enforcement means that some underage drinkers can still obtain alcohol with relative ease— minimum age of purchase could still affect youth homicide as a proxy for youth-specific consumption.

Even in the lax enforcement scenario, not all enforcement would be lax, and the opportunity costs for underage drinkers to obtain alcoholic beverages do increase. Thus the model depicted in figure 6.1 includes a fully specified consumption equation, including minimum age of purchase as a predictor. Minimum age of purchase could have indirect effects on homicide through consumption, as well as a direct effect. If the notion that minimum drinking age only impacts homicide indirectly through consumption is true, then it will be the case that the direct effect of minimum age of purchase on homicide shown in figure 6.1 will be indistinguishable from zero.

If the impact of minimum age of purchase on consumption is appropriately modeled only in the context of a comprehensive model of consumption, then the same is true for the impact of minimum age of purchase on youth homicide. Only in the context of a comprehensive model of homicide could this effect be appropriately evaluated. Figure 6.1 summarizes the implication of this discussion, as it displays a two-equation system in which consumption is regressed on a set of predictors, including minimum age of purchase, and youth homicide is regressed on a set of predictors, including both minimum age of purchase and consumption.

A final unaddressed question concerns the predictors of both homicide and consumption that should be included, beyond what was included in the analysis reported in chapter 5. For youth homicide, measures to be added to the analysis include two of the variables that total population may have proxied for in the analysis presented here, proportion young people and proportion living in urban areas (Hirschi and Gottfredson, 1983; Smith and Parker, 1980). In addition to better measures of inequality, unemployment should also be considered (Parker and Toth, 1990). Finally, homicide sanctions, like capital punishment rates and sentence lengths for homicide offenders, should also be considered, as these represent direct crime control policies that were being used more frequently during the period to be studied here. Unless these measures are included, minimum age of purchase could be acting as a proxy for crime control policy changes that are unmeasured in the model analyzed in chapter 5 (Bowers, 1984; Bailey and Peterson, 1989; Bailey, 1990).

In addition to the minimum age of purchase, what other predictors of consumption should be included? Economic factors, such as price, taxation rates, and income, tourism volume, whether the state has monopoly control on retail sales or distribution of alcohol, percent urban, proportion young people, and unemployment have all been used successfully in models of aggregate alcohol consumption (Ponicki, 1990 for a review).

The degree of overlap in these two literature is not surprising, given the results of the analyses presented here. Alcohol is linked to homicide, and therefore it should not be surprising if they had some common determinants. The study that has been described here is currently underway, having been funded in late 1993 by the National Institute on Alcohol Abuse and Alcoholism. This study should result in a complete and comprehensive understanding of the impact of minimum age of purchase policy changes during the 1980s on both youth homicide and consumption of alcohol. It should serve to clarify the nature of the relationship between alcohol and homicide.

Unasked and Unanswered: Additional
Issues Regarding Availability and Violence

The analysis of city alcohol availability and homicide presented and discussed in chapter 4 is, because of limitations of data available for a national study at three points in time, unable to address a number of important issues concerning this relationship. One very important and potentially interesting one is whether availability and violence are linked not only within relatively large and heterogeneous units like cities, but also at a much finer-grained level of analysis. At the block or neighborhood level, it is much more credible to assert that when availability and violence happen in the same physical space, they are indeed related to each other. Another way to state the question is whether or not alcohol availability and violence are causally linked across space, or do they simply happen to occur near one another because of common causes, such as were described above in the discussion of the new research project on minimum age, consumption, and youth homicide? Is it coincidental, or is there a significant relationship behind the fact, that parts of cities where the alcohol outlet density is extremely high are also places that frequently come to the attention of law enforcement and community residents as the location of violent crimes?

A study designed to examine this spatially based question about the link between availability and violence is one in which the initial data collection links the known addresses of alcohol outlets in a community with the known addresses, locations, intersections, parks, and so on, where law enforcement personnel are called to investigate violent incidents. Once the exact locations are converted so that they can be read by geobased computer software, computerized maps showing the spatial overlap between violence and alcohol outlets can be produced. More importantly, a variety of spatially based coefficients, which express the link between variables in terms of distance, can be calculated and subjected to spatially adapted statistical techniques (Cliff and Ord, 1973; Loftin and Ward, 1983; Griffith, 1988; Anselin, 1988). The analysis of this relationship can also be subjected to a reasonably long list of socioeconomic conditions thought to produce both violence and outlet concentration, as data for census tracts, units with about 2,500 to 8,000 residents, and block groups, which are the subunits of census tracts, the former having about 100 to 1,000 people, are available from U.S. Census Bureau sources. This more fine-grained analysis of city availability and violence will allow for a more direct examination of the assumption that because there is a relationship between availability and homicide, this can be taken to support the idea that alcohol helps to cause homicide.

Given the precision in this design, a number of other aspects of violence, to date unasked and therefore unanswered in research, can also be addressed. The study as designed is focused on youth violence and alcohol outlet density in Mexican-American neighborhoods, in part because so little is known about violence in the Mexican-American community specifically or, more generally, in the Latino community in the United States. In addition, because the Mexican-American community in the United States is one of the largest and most clearly identified, both by Mexican-Americans themselves and by others, alcohol advertisers and producers have engaged in a campaign of concentrated targeting and promotion of alcohol products in this community (Maxwell and Jacobson, 1989). This project will include an observational study of the nature, content, and volume of alcohol advertising in Mexican-American neighborhoods. It will include variables derived from this observational data collection effort in the analysis of the relationship between outlet density and youth violence. As was the case with minimum age of purchase, it may be that such advertising has a direct effect on youth violence in the Mexican-American community, due perhaps to the objectification of women or the glorification of violent sports, or through some other mechanism. This is the first study we are aware of that attempts to link violence to outlet density and culturally related targeting in advertisement and promotion of alcoholic beverages. It is also currently underway, having been funded in late 1993 by a private foundation, the California Wellness Foundation of Woodland Hills, California (Alaniz and Parker, 1993).

Differentiating the Role of Alcohol for the Victim of Violence

Routine activity and the lifestyle approach, discussed in some detail in chapter 2, are both based in part on the recognition that certain structural and individual conditions can either raise or lower the relative risk that a particular individual will become a victim of violence. Although both the analyses presented here use victim-based rates of homicide as dependent variables, these rates are treated as indicators of a homicide event in both cases. For the purpose of macrolevel analyses like these, there is no particular theoretical reason to focus on either the victim or the offender, and individual level studies of victims and offenders show that they are usually very similar in terms of demographic variables like age, racial or ethnic group, and place of residence. It is often hard to tell, other than by who dies and who survives, which individual is to be designated as the victim and which is the offender (Lauretsen et al., 1991). However, it may be the case that one of the things that differentiates the victim from the offender is if and how much alcohol is present in each participant, as it may be that the eventual victim is the one most incapacitated by the effects of alcohol.

Most studies of alcohol and violence have focused on the offender, an approach that results in a number of difficulties for the scientific study of homicide, or any form of violence for that matter, and alcohol (Pernanen, 1981, 1991; Collins, 1981; Murdoch et al., 1990). Given that the victim and offender distinction is often post hoc, a focus exclusively on those who have been labeled offenders after the fact seems misguided, and as Collins (1983, 1989) has suggested, a focus on those labeled as victims post hoc might reveal a great deal more about the influence of alcohol on the risk of being involved in a violent act than a focus on offender drinking alone. After all, one could have a perfectly sober offender and an intoxicated victim, and it would still be reasonable to look for the causal role of alcohol in the violent incident represented by these circumstances. Evidence from the British crime victim survey (Gottfredson, 1984) shows that drinkers were three times more likely to have been victimized than nondrinkers, controlling for age and place of residence. There is both empirical and theoretical evidence to suggest the importance of examining the alcohol and violence link through research on victim risk factors.

However, one of the problems in studying victims, like that which occurs when studying offenders, is the lack of an appropriate comparison group with which to compare the experiences and behaviors of the victims. If one is studying offenders, for example, and finds that 75 percent of the offenders drank alcohol before committing their offenses, the temptation is great to claim that alcohol has a major influence on offending behavior. However, if it is the case that 85 percent of the nonoffenders also drank alcohol at the same time as the offenders, the role of alcohol as a causal agent in offending is suspect. Similarly, in any study of victims, a comparative sample of nonvictims with similar demographic characteristics, who are also asked about their drinking behavior, would go a long way toward insuring that the appropriate inferences about the role of alcohol in victimization can be made.

Designing a study on alcohol consumption and victimization risk also affords a very good opportunity to extend the measurement of routine activity in a significant way. Most studies that have examined the link between routine activity and either victimization or crime have used generic measures of routine activities, such as survey questions about the number of nights or days per week that a person is out of the home (Miethe et al., 1987; Maxfield, 1987; Sampson and Wooldredge, 1987). Other studies have relied on indirect measures of household structure and activities, such as measures like female labor force participation and retail eating and drinking places used here in chapter 4, or the household activity ratio or other measures of household structure used in a number of studies (Cohen and Felson, 1979; Smith and Jarjoura, 1988; Treno, Parker, and Holder, 1993). Linking the measurement of routine activity to routine alcohol-related behavior would add a great deal of precision to the measurement of this key concept.

A study designed to address these issues related to the link between alcohol and victim risk is currently underway, having been funded in late 1992 by NIAAA as part of a national research center grant to the Prevention Research Center in Berkeley, California. The project involves data collection from two samples, one consisting of the robbery and assault victims for which official police reports are available in a medium-sized United States city. The second sample is a rolling, demographically matched sample, collected as part of a larger, representative sample of the same United States city. A rolling sample design is used for the comparison sample, as the victim interviews will generate between fifty to seventy-five respondents per month, and will continue for three years in order to generate sufficient cases for adequate statistical power. This fact means that we can build the comparison sample gradually over time, with continuous adjustment of the demographics of the comparisons to match the potentially changing demographics of the victim sample. Respondents to both samples will be asked detailed questions about their routine alcohol-related behaviors, and they will be asked to describe their behaviors at places and times, for the victim sample, that relate to the victimization event and, for the comparison sample, times and places that match the times and places when and where victimizations happened.

This careful construction of the basis for comparison between victims and nonvictims should allow for a more valid inference about the role of alcohol consumption in the violent victimizations to be studied, which include robberies, muggings, purse snatching, and nonsexual assaults of various types. The addition of a number of questions about alcohol-related behavior, questions that are not available on surveys such as the National Crime Victim Survey (U.S. Bureau of Justice Statistics, 1992), will also reveal the degree to which routine activities of alcohol are significant factors in determining the relative risk of violent victimization.

Unaddressed Questions of Policy:
Other Strategies to Reduce Alcohol-Related Violence

Serious effort in the current study has been directed toward evaluation of a policy change that previously occurred, increases in the minimum age of purchase for alcohol, in terms of its impact on youth homicide, and considerably more effort will be devoted to this topic in one of the new, ongoing projects described in this chapter. Many of those interested in policy change directed toward the prevention and control of alcohol-related violence however, may be less than enthusiastic—after all, this policy change has already occurred, and we still have rising rates of youth homicide. It is all very well to gain experience from a complete understanding of how past policy changes have affected alcohol-related violence, but there is a greater imperative for the design, implementation, and evaluation of future policy strategies design to break or at least further weaken the alcohol and violence link.

It should be pointed out, however, as a minor but important cautionary, that it was only just over twenty years ago when minimum drinking ages were lowered in a number of states without much knowledge or consideration of the consequences for young people in particular and society as a whole. It is therefore worthwhile to fully document the positive impact of an increase in the minimum age of purchase, especially in terms of an unanticipated outcome like youth homicide. This line of research does, however, set the stage for the obvious follow-up question: If one kind of alcohol-control measure has an effect on violence prevention, are there any other candidates in the alcohol-prevention field that might also have similar effects on violence?

One answer to this question is implied by the fine-grained analysis of outlet density and youth violence in the Mexican-American community described previously. The planning and zoning regulations in place in many communities throughout the United States contain provisions that would allow local communities to regulate the density and location of alcohol outlets, if such communities were convinced that these businesses could pose a threat to public order and community safety. These provisions are usually described as conditional use permits (Whittman and Hilton, 1987; Holder, 1989a). In many cases, these provisions may not only be used to deny permits to certain types of business in certain locations, but they can also be used to regulate hours and other business practices of establishments. In most places these provisions are used very infrequently, and usually with regard to issues like the location of a pornographic bookstore or movie theater near a school. These provisions, however, could be used to regulate alcohol availability, once the evidence to be collected in the density and youth violence project described here, and others like it, can be assembled and disseminated (presuming that such evidence does indeed show that there is valid cause to claim a casual link between outlet concentration and violence in small areas).

Another area of potential promise is the area of server intervention, responsible beverage service, and dram shop liability as a way of directly regulating or modifying the practices of outlets that serve alcohol for on-site consumption (Saltz, 1986, 1987, 1993). Server intervention and responsible beverage service include the implementation through the training of alcohol servers in commercial establishments to avoid serving additional alcohol to customers who show outward signs of impairment, avoiding practices such as double bubble and other promotional strategies that encourage high volume consumption over a short period of time, offering food to customers in bars, and restricting the sale of large quantity servings of alcohol, like pitchers of beer or mixed drinks, to single individuals. These practices have been shown to be effective in reducing intoxication rates among bar patrons in two studies of different types of on-site outlets (Saltz and Hennessy, 1990a, 1990b). But what is the link between server intervention and violence? If there is a link, how, short of draconian on-site outlet regulation (which would be heavily opposed by the alcohol industry as well as by outlet owners and workers), can this approach help in the design of policy strategies aimed at reducing alcohol-related violence?

The potential link of serving practices to violence is not as far fetched as some may assume. Ample evidence that there is a link between bars and other outlets and calls to the police to respond to violent crimes is found in a newly developing area of criminological research referred to as hot spots of crime. In an investigation of the places that police were repeatedly called to in a large United States city, on-site outlets such as bars and restaurants were among the hottest spots in the data (Sherman et al., 1989).

For example, the top hot spot between December 1985 and December 1986 in the city examined was an intersection where there were several bars, a liquor store, and a park. Police received 33 calls reporting rapes, robberies, and auto thefts during the year observed in these data. The third-ranking hot spot, with 27 such calls, was another intersection with several bars; the fifth- and sixth-hottest locations, 27 and 25 calls, respectively, also involved multiple or, in the case of the sixth-hot spot, a single on-site alcohol outlet. In fact, Sherman et al. (1989: 45) report that on-site alcohol outlets were part of the locations that accounted for one-third of the robberies, rapes, and auto thefts reported in the course of a year. Sherman et al. (1989: 44) report that the sixth-hottest spot in the city, an individual bar, had a robbery rate that was seven times the robbery rate of the entire city, and a rate of one assault for every four persons who visited the bar during the year, assuming maximum occupancy during open hours.

The theoretical development of selective disinhibition, and the review of cases from Wilbanks (1984) in light of selective disinhibition, combined with the data from Sherman et al. (1989) should leave no doubt as to the theoretical possibility that what goes on in bars and restaurants with regard to alcohol consumption and server practices is related to the violence that police end up being called to deal with. It is also well known from victimization surveys that the police deal with somewhere between one-half and one-third of all the violent incidents that individuals report being involved in (Parker, 1994a), so it is likely that even the hot spots data underestimate the link between alcohol and violence at or near on-site alcohol outlets. This opens the potential, therefore, for research designed to evaluate the efficacy of server intervention and training programs to reduce violence and, as a measurable manifestation of such reductions, repeat calls to police for violent incidents at such on-site alcohol outlets.

Even the admiring skeptic might wonder how bar owners and managers would be convinced to take part in such programs, even if they could be convinced that violence associated with their establishments would be reduced, given that server intervention may be perceived as cutting into the profit margin of such establishments by lowering overall consumption. If conditional use permits were considered on the basis of criteria like repeat calls to the police from a location, this might be one incentive. Another more positive incentive would be to offer reduced costs to owners through less expensive group dram shop liability insurance, offered through the coordination

of local officials, to all establishments that take part in server training and maintain responsible beverage service practices (Saltz, 1993).
A research project is in the proposal development stage in late 1993
that would at least provide an answer to the question of whether
server intervention can be shown to be related to violence that happens in or near on-site alcohol outlets. This would be a first step
toward designing a more widely implemented public policy designed
to put this type of intervention into place. As was the case with the
minimum age of purchase laws, evidence is beginning to show that
server intervention can reduce risk of drunk driving. Given the link
to the hot spots of violence discussed here, it is again legitimate to
ask if such alcohol-related interventions may also have an impact on
violence reduction or prevention.

ALCOHOL AND HOMICIDE: A FEW FINAL WORDS

The ongoing and planned research projects described here
have some common themes based on the efforts and accomplish-
ments of the current study of alcohol and homicide that has been
the subject of this book. First, the new projects all pursue the goal
of greater precision: precision in measurement, precision in the
theoretical and empirical assessment of the alcohol and violence
link, precision in terms of interventions that move closer to the
actual occurrence of alcohol-related violence. These new studies
also pursue additional information on the nature of the relationships observed in the current study: the meaning of race and ethnic
differences in violence, alcohol and other factors; the importance of
spatial relationships between where violence occurs and where
alcohol is sold and consumed; the further evaluation of policy
designed to control alcohol with regard to the impact on violence;
and implications of context, physical and social, for the alcohol
and violence relationship.

Finally, these new studies share in common with the results
presented here a desire to push the theoretical understanding of the
relationship between violence and alcohol to the greatest extent
possible, and to link such understanding to research that not only
tests the validity of the theory, but links both theory and data to
the design of interventions that may reduce the level of alcohol-
related violence. As the present results and the descriptions of these

new projects show, this is not an easy task, nor is it at all clear that it will be ultimately successful. But the evidence presented here shows that there is some promise in this pursuit. Given the importance of the goal—violence reduction and prevention—this task is surely worth the time, money, and effort that we will devote to it.

METHODOLOGICAL AND STATISTICAL ISSUES FOR
ANALYSES PRESENTED IN CHAPTERS 4 AND 5

This appendix describes the approach taken in the estimation of structural equation and pooled cross section time series models, results of which are presented in chapters 4 and 5. A general philosophical approach to modeling, especially with regard to the structural equation models present in chapter 4, is followed by a description of the base line structural equation model and the modifications made to that base line model to arrive at the results presented earlier. The structure of the interaction models is summarized, followed by a description of the approach used in the pooled cross section time series models presented in chapter 5. The impact of pooling is discussed in general, and the specific techniques used to address this impact are reported, as well as an investigation of floor effects in the pooled models presented here. Appendix 2, which contains a list of the cities included in the analyses of chapter 4, and the means and standard deviations for both data sets, follows immediately after Appendix 1.

A Philosophy of Structural Equation Modeling: One Approach

In labeling what is to follow a *philosophy*, and *one approach*, it is recognized that the state of structural equation modeling is still as much an *art* as it is a science. Programs such as EQS 4 for Windows

(Bentler and Wu, 1993) are still rather difficult to use, and require a great deal of experience to be mastered. In addition, as the moniker *one approach* suggests, expert practitioners disagree, sometimes in the most basic way, about how best to estimate a complex structural model. In chapters 3 and 4 hints to the complexity of the basic structural model used here were made, and in this appendix a more precise discussion of the nature of these models is given. This is by no means required reading for those who want to understand the results that have been presented. This material is presented for the technically minded and experienced structural equation modeler, who wants to learn more about how these results were generated. I will not offer much in the way of justification for my approach to structural equation modeling, as I believe it to represent some of the common wisdom about how such things are done, but I want to describe it in enough detail so that the technically adept reader knows what I did to produce the results reported here. Such readers may have different approaches, and may disagree with some of what I have done. If so, I invite them to take up keyboard, mouse, and structural equation program and join the debate.

Considering the basic model presented in chapter 4, two major issues were of concern in constructing that model. First, the issue of longitudinal, statistical control in the analysis of change in homicide, alcohol availability, and the remaining variables considered, was of paramount importance. There is simply no other approach that enables the analyst to understand the change and stability in the structural relationships being modeled. The second issue involved the way theoretical and empirical information were utilized in the specification of the model. The primary information used was theoretical and logical—that is, How should the model look from a theoretical and a logical perspective? However, once the first model was estimated, empirical information based on the diagnostics available in EQS4 for Windows (residuals, indices of fit, la grange multiplier tests; see Bentler and Wu, 1993) provided an additional set of information to base respecification of the model upon. The basic structure of the model was thus based on these two major issues, control and specification information from the two sources.

This basic structure is presented in figure A1-1, which gives the basic form of the equations used to estimate the baseline model. As can be seen in figure A1-1, the base line model involved thirty-four variables, twelve in each decade (the regional indicator did not change during the period, thus there are thirty-four variables instead of thirty-six, but there are eleven net effects of independent variables on homicide estimated for each decade, plus two additional effects of previous decade's homicide on current decade's homicide for the 1970 and 1980 decades). The three equations for homicide in 1960, 1970, and 1980 represent the most important part of the model, and were the subject of all but one of the tables in chapter 4. However, as shown here, twenty additional equations were required to properly specify the stability and change model. These equations represent the effects of previous observations on the independent variables on current independent variables, making it possible to assess stability, the effect of previous observations on present observations of the same variable, and change, the impact of the change in an independent variable on the change in the dependent variable. When this kind of model is specified, the effect parameters are in fact change effects, as they are interpreted as the effect of X_1 on Y_1, given that the effects of X_0 on X_1 and Y_0 on Y_1 have been controlled. If X_0 and X_1 or Y_0 and Y_1 were perfectly correlated—that is, there was no change or, put another way, there was perfect stability—there would be nothing for X_1 to explain in Y_1. However, without control for X_0 and Y_0, the nature of any effect estimated between X_1 and Y_1 cannot be determined uniquely. Such an effect could be the result of changes in X_1 causing changes in Y_1, or the result of a noncausal process. For example, if X_0 and Y_0 were unrelated, but the value of Y rose uniformly between time 0 and time 1, while the value of X remained the same between time periods, X_1 and Y_1 would appear to be causally related at time 1. Controlling for time 0 in both variables would reveal that X was stable, and thus could not have caused changes in Y between times 0 and 1. This ability to distinguish stability and change is the key feature of the approach taken here to modeling the relationship between availability, homicide, and the other variables included.

What is not shown in figure A1-1 is the fact that the error terms for homicide in 1970 and 1980 were correlated. This is an essential feature of the model, and a failure to correlate these error terms would be a major specification error. Correlated error terms of equations normally represented omitted variables that two dependent variables have in common, and it is obviously the case that homicide in 1970 and homicide in 1980 would have common omitted variables. However, in the longitudinal model being specified here, the error terms are correlated by virtue of the over time relationship of the two dependent measures. This is referred to as serial or auto-correlation, and the model would be badly misspecified if this correlation were not accounted for.

The original specification, based on a theoretically derived set of information, was concerned with which variables should be included so as to derive appropriate net estimates of the effects in the model. The basic model was also restricted logically, so that initially only effects of independent variables on homicide at the same time period—that is, 1960 poverty was specified as affecting 1960 homicide—not 1970 or 1980 homicide. In addition, the stability equations were also restricted initially to poverty in 1960 affecting poverty in 1970, but not in 1980. Other variables were also restricted, so that median age in 1960 was not allowed to affect poverty in 1970. However, it is here that empirical information became useful. As reported in chapter 4, the initial model, so specified, did not fit the data in an acceptable manner. Some modifications were called for, as until a structural model fits the data reasonably well (more about the philosophy of fit adopted here will be presented below), the results cannot be interpreted with any confidence.

It is at this juncture that many experienced analysts part company as to how to proceed. The approach taken here was an empirical one, so that if the diagnostic tests indicated that estimating a certain restricted relationship in the model would lead to a significant improvement in the fit of the model, that path was included in the specification and the model reestimated, in the absence of any particular theoretical rationale, as long as two conditions were met. First, the new parameter could not be contrary to logic—that is, the impact of poverty in 1980 affecting the age structure in 1970. In addition, the relationship could not be contrary to theory—that is, the homicide rate in 1970 affecting the poverty rate in 1970. Other than these restrictions, any relationship indicated by the diagnostics was included, and remained part of the model as long as it resulted in significant improvement in model fit when it was first included.

Figure A1-2 gives the modified model, which also included some additional correlated errors of equations, reflecting the common omitted variables situation described previously or a strong pattern of serial correlation over time among the stability estimates for the independent variables: migration in 1980 with income in 1970; social bonds in 1980 with social bonds in 1970; and age in

1980 with age in 1970. As serial correlation is a more serious problem for the dependent variable, these latter correlated error terms were only added if there was diagnostic information suggesting that significant fit improvement would result.

In summary, it should be noted that the specification of the final models for chapter 4 is a result of theoretical and empirical information, leading to a model that fits the data relatively well, and whose parameters are relatively stable. During the last five runs, the substantively interesting parameters were monitored carefully to ascertain if the relatively minor changes being made in the structure of the model were having a large impact on the parameters and their standard errors. To much relief it was found that the estimates presented in chapter 4 were relatively stable as the final model was approached.

As far as determining when to stop, two criteria were used. First, the diagnostic tests for the final models show no additional parameter, which was logically possible, even under the relaxed rules described above, and which would add significantly to the fit of the model. Second, some potential parameters seemed to be close to adding to the fit, according to the diagnostics, and several of these were tried empirically and found to be insignificant themselves, to have no impact on overall model fit, and to have no impact on the other parameters in the model.

An issue related to these stopping rules is that of the definition of *reasonably* good fit. In chapter 4 a number of fit indicators are reported, including the chi-square test, goodness of fit index, and the explained variance for each homicide equation. According to a strict interpretation of the chi-square test, none of the models reported here fit the observed data. Some models, due to their structure, and to the type of data they are built on, will not ever fit the observations according to this criterion. For example, there is no measurement model associated with the structural model under consideration here. If we had multiple indicators for each variable within decade, the fit of the overall model could probably be achieved by correlated measurement errors across time and between indicators. Probably some of the empirically justified modifications added between figure A1-1 and figure A1-2 reflect common measurement error, although there is no way to tell from these results. In addition, there are plenty of parameters that are logically constrained to zero in this model, which, if estimated, would lead to a nonsignificant chi-square test. However, the good-ness of fit index, adjusted for degrees of freedom, is an alterna-tive way of judging relative fit, and those values as presented in chapter 4 suggest that these models fit the observed data reason-ably well.

The interaction models presented in chapter 4 were constructed in a similar manner. As no new variables were being added, but combinations of information already in these data, the interaction terms were added to the final base line model as given in figure A1-2 (plus the correlated error terms previously described). Diagnostic information was monitored to see if any additional modifications to the models were required, but none were found that would have improved the fit or conformed with the logic of this model. Two additional equations were included, these being the 1970 and 1980 stability equations for each interaction term.

Pooled Cross Section Time Series Models of Chapter 5

The file structure required for a pooled cross section time series analysis is somewhat unusual. The data are arrayed first by cross section—that is, states—and within each cross section by time. An example of this structure would be:

Alabama$_{76}$	primary homicide$_{76}$	infant mortality$_{76}$
Alabama$_{77}$	primary homicide$_{77}$	infant mortality$_{77}$
Alabama$_{78}$	primary homicide$_{78}$	infant mortality$_{78}$
Alabama$_{83}$	primary homicide$_{83}$	infant mortality$_{83}$
Alaska$_{76}$	primary homicide$_{76}$	infant mortality$_{76}$
Alaska$_{83}$	primary homicide$_{83}$	infant mortality$_{83}$
Arkansas$_{76}$	primary homicide$_{76}$	infant mortality$_{76}$

This type of file structure requires statistical analysis with soft-ware designed to recognize and deal effectively with this type of file structure, for by nature pooled cross section time series designs vio-late a number of the statistical assumptions of standard techniques. The appropriate statistical model is an approach referred to as Generalized Least Squares (GLS), the advantages of which are dis-cussed below. However, it is important to note here that the degrees of freedom for this analysis are obtained by multiplying the number of cross sections (51) times the number of time points (8), for a total of 408 *cases* in the analysis. This result comes about because each year by state data point is treated as an observation in pooled cross section time series analysis.

This pooling creates several statistical problems that make conventional regression models untenable, thus requiring particular statistical treatment if unbiased and efficient estimates are to be obtained. First, pooled data violates the assumption of independence across observations that is a major requisite of OLS (ordinary least squares or regression) analysis. The fact that each variable consists of repeated measurements of the same state over time creates an over time or serial dependence, which in turn causes the residuals to be skewed and estimates of the standard errors of regression coefficients to be seriously underestimated, a very dangerous source of type II error resulting in the false finding of an effect when no effect exists (Stimson, 1985).

The second problem confronted by analysts of pooled data has its origins in the cross-sectional aspect of the data, rather than in the time series aspect. The assumption of homoscedasticity, or equal variances across all cases, is often a problem in OLS analyses, but this problem is exacerbated in the pooled case. If one of the fifty-one states has much larger or smaller variance than the rest, in a pooled model that unit contributes T cases with extreme variance to the overall database, where T is equal to the number of time points. This violation of the assumption of equal variances across levels of the dependent variable leads to estimates that are inefficient—that is, with standard errors overestimated (Stimson, 1985). Thus the problem of heteroscedasticity is likely to produce more damage to pooled estimates than to OLS estimates, because of the nature of the data structure in the former case.

It would be fortunate if these two sources of problems for the estimation of standard error would cancel each other out, but in fact the combination of autocorrelation and heteroscedasticity in analyses using pooled data interact to produce a third, and even more dangerous, problem. In cases where the number of cross-sectional units is greater than the number of time points, as is the case in the proposed research, estimates of the effect parameters will be biased as well as potentially inefficient. The standard diagnostic tests used in regression analysis will indicate that autocorrelation is very large. However, the actual problem is one of the combination of these two violations, and using corrections for autocorrelation (to be discussed below) will leave the estimates obtained both biased and inefficient (Stimson, 1985:919-21).

Appropriate statistical models can be estimated, however, with a Generalized Least Squares (GLS) approach designed to control for the impact of these problems (Stimson, 1985, for a thorough and accessible discussion). Particular equations tend to be dominated by either cross-sectional heteroscedasticity or by time serial autocorrelation, with the form of the GLS correction depending on which type of problem is dominant. Appropriate diagnosis of the dominant source of inefficiency and bias is thus crucial to the estimation of the proper pooled cross-sectional time series model. Fortunately, standard residual diagnosis techniques can be utilized in an iterative procedure to determine the appropriate statistical form of the model. First, an OLS regression model is estimated with the pooled data. The autocorrelations and partial autocorrelations for the first five time lags are examined, much in the same manner as these diagnostics are used in conventional time series analysis (O'Malley and Wagenaar, 1991), except that the interpretation is somewhat different. If the autocorrelations display a pattern of nonlinear decay, with a very significant value at time lag 1, a sharply lower value at lag 2, going to zero or even negative by lags 3, 4, and 5, this indicative of a process dominated by time serial autocorrelation. The general form of the GLS model is given in equation 1, and the correction for this statistical form is given in equations 2 and 2a:

$$\beta = [X'\Omega^{-1}X]^{-1}X'\Omega^{-1}Y \tag{1}$$

where β = a vector of effect parameters
  Ω = generalized least squares correction matrix
  X = a vector of exogenous variables
  Y = an endogenous variable

$$\Omega = \begin{matrix} \sigma_1^2\,A & O & \ldots & O \\ O & \sigma_2^2\,A & \ldots & O \\ \ldots & \ldots & \ldots & \ldots \\ O & O & \ldots & \sigma_n^2\,A \end{matrix} \tag{2}$$

where $\sigma_i^2\,A$ = unique error variance for each cross section

$$
A = \begin{matrix}
1 & \rho & \rho^2 & \ldots & \rho^{t-1} \\
\rho & 1 & \rho & \ldots & \rho^{t-2} \\
\ldots & \ldots & \ldots & \ldots & \ldots \\
\rho^{t-1} & \ldots & \rho^2 & \ldots & 1
\end{matrix} \qquad (2a)
$$

where ρ = first order autocorrelation coefficient
t = the number of time points

The structure of the matrix A, in which the autocorrelation parameters decline geometrically at each successively longer lag, is consistent with the autoregressive model indicated by the residual autocorrelations. The fact that the GLS correction matrix also allows for a unique variance for each cross section also means that heteroscedasticity can be corrected simultaneously in the process of correcting for autocorrelation, although this correction works well only if the data are time serially dominated.

In the case where the data are dominated by cross-sectional heteroscedasticity, the interpretation of the residual autocorrelations is complicated by the fact that this heteroscedasticity manifests itself in the diagnostics in the same manner a more complicated time serial model would in a conventional time series analysis (Stimson, 1985: 920). It is the pooled nature of the data that produce such a pattern of autocorrelations—no decay, out to lags 3, 4, or even 5—when cross-sectional error variance is dominant over time serial variance. Equations 3a and 3b give the form of the GLS correction matrix in this case:

$$
\Omega = \sigma^2 \begin{bmatrix}
A & O & \ldots & O \\
O & A & \ldots & O \\
\ldots & O & A & \ldots \\
O & O & \ldots & A
\end{bmatrix} \qquad (3a)
$$

where σ^2 = the overall variance for the model

$$
A = \begin{bmatrix}
1 & \rho & \rho & \ldots & \rho \\
\rho & 1 & \rho & \ldots & \rho \\
\ldots & \ldots & \ldots & \ldots & \ldots \\
\rho & \ldots & \rho & \ldots & 1
\end{bmatrix} \qquad (3b)
$$

where ρ = the overall unit specific correction factor

Unlike the time serial case, in which the correction factor is estimated from the OLS residuals, the error components case, as this
approach is termed (Stimson, 1985:922-25; Nerlove, 1971; Maddala,
1971), requires a two-step procedure for the estimation of the correction factor. As the correction factor is essentially a summary of
the unit specific effects, it is estimated by a decomposition of the
overall residual term. This is accomplished by first estimating an
OLS equation, followed by an OLS equation that includes a dummy
variable for each unit. This latter approach, referred to as Least
Squares with Dummy Variables (LSDV) (Stimson, 1985:921-22), is a
saturated model with regard to cross-sectional variation. It has a
number of undesirable properties, including the fact that the large
number of dummy variables it entails (51 in the current case) will
often cause collinearity with the remaining predictors in the equation and are themselves uninterpretable from a substantive point of
view. However, by subtracting the within variance estimate of the
LSDV from the OLS regression, and taking the result as a proportion
of the total variance, a summary measure of the variance due to
unique cross-sectional effects—that is, heteroscedasticity—can be
generated and utilized in the formation of the GLS correction matrix
given in equation 3b.

In either the time serial or the cross-sectional dominated case,
some variation due to the less dominant process—due to time serial
effects in the cross-sectional model, or due to cross-sectional effects
in the time serial model—may remain as significant sources of bias
and inefficiency. An examination of the residual variances from the
two GLS models can reveal such a problem. A small number of
dummy variables representing the time or unit specific effects can be
added to either model without difficulty.

The Particular Application of
Pooled Cross Section Modeling for Chapter 5

Having presented a general discussion of the problems caused by
pooling cross sections and time series together, the particular specification of the models reported in chapter 5 can be presented. In the
case of the results reported in table 5.1, the primary homicide equations were found to be dominated by over time error correlations,
thus requiring an AR(1) or Auto Regressive lag one time period (year)
correction factor used in equation 2a. However, the nonprimary

homicide equations displayed a different pattern of errors as a result of pooling, and were found to be dominated by cross-sectional variation. LSDV models were estimated, and the results of these and the OLS models were used to calculate the correction factor to be plugged into equation 3b. In each case, the exact value of the correction factor in each equation is given in table 5.1. It should also be noted that both GLS specifications make the conventionally calculated explained variance or R^2 measure inaccurate, thus explaining the use of OLS regression explained variance results in table 5.1.

In addition, *floor effects* were found to be a problem in this analysis, especially for the three primary homicide equations, as four states in particular had almost no primary homicides during this period (North Dakota, West Virginia, South Dakota, and Vermont). The impact of ignoring floor effects can be severe, especially in the case of a pooled model in which each unit that suffers from the problem contributes multiple cases to the analysis. There are two approaches to handling floor effects, and in the results reported here, these effects are controlled by including a dummy variable in each of the three primary homicide equations for the four states (these coefficients are not reported in table 5.1). One can also exclude the zero or near zero cases from the analysis, but in this case the results of the exclusion approach are identical to those reported in Table 5.1, and this latter procedure is not recommended due to the loss of degrees of freedom it represents.

HOMICIDE60 = AGE60 + FEMALE LABOR FORCE PARTICIPATION60
+ INCOME60 + %KIDS WITH ONE PARENT60 + MIGRATION60
+ DENSITY60 + RACIAL COMPOSITION60 + REGION +
EATING/DRINKING ACTIVITY60($) + ALCOHOL
AVAILABILITY60 + SOCIAL BONDS60 + E1

HOMICIDE70 = HOMICIDE60 + AGE70 + FEMALE LABOR FORCE
PARTICIPATION70 + INCOME70 + %KIDS WITH ONE
PARENT70 + MIGRATION70 + DENSITY70 + RACIAL
COMPOSITION70 + REGION + EATING/DRINKING
ACTIVITY70($) + ALCOHOL AVAILABILITY70 + SOCIAL
BONDS70 + E13

AGE70 = AGE60 + E14 ;
FEMALE LABOR FORCE PARTICIPATION70 = FEMALE LABOR
FORCE PARTICIPATION60 + E15 ;
INCOME70 = INCOME60 + E16 ;
%KIDS WITH ONE PARENT70 = %KIDS WITH ONE PARENT60 + E17 ;
MIGRATION70 = MIGRATION60 + E18 ;
DENSITY70 = DENSITY60 + E19 ;
RACIAL COMP0STION70 = RACIAL COMPOSITION60 + E20 ;
EATING/DRINKING ACTIVITY($)70 = EATING/DRINKING
ACTIVITY60($) + E21 ;
ALCOHOL AVAILABILITY70 = ALCOHOL AVAILABILITY60 + E22 ;
SOCIAL BONDS70 = SOCIAL BONDS60 + E23 ;

HOMICIDE80 = HOMICIDE70 + AGE80 + FEMALE LABOR FORCE
PARTICIPATION80 + INCOME80 + %KIDS WITH ONE
PARENT80 + MIGRATION80 + DENSITY80 + RACIAL
COMPOSITION80 + REGION + EATING/DRINKING
ACTIVITY80($) + ALCOHOL AVAILABILITY80 + SOCIAL
BONDS80 + E24 ;

AGE80 = AGE70 + E25 ;
FEMALE LABOR FORCE PARTICIPATION80 = FEMALE LABOR
FORCE PARTICIPATION70 + E26 ;
INCOME80 = INCOME70 + E27 ;
%KIDS WITH ONE PARENT80 = %KIDS WITH ONE PARENT70 + E28 ;

(continued on next page)

MIGRATION80 = MIGRATION70 + E29 ;
DENSITY80 = DENSITY70 + E30 ;
RACIAL COMPOSITION80 = RACIAL COMPOSITION70 + E31 ;
EATING/DRINKING ACTIVITY80($) = EATING/DRINKING
    ACTIVITY70($) + E32 ;
ALCOHOL AVAILABILITY80 = ALCOHOL AVAILABILITY70 + E33 ;
SOCIAL BONDS80 = SOCIAL BONDS70 + E34 ;

FIGURE A1-2
Base Line Model, Chapter 4, with Modifications

HOMICIDE60 = AGE60 + FEMALE LABOR FORCE PARTICIPATION60
    + INCOME60 + %KIDS WITH ONE PARENT60 + MIGRATION60
    + DENSITY60 + RACIAL COMPOSITION60 + REGION +
    EATING/DRINKING ESTABLISHMENTS60+ ALCOHOL
    AVAILABILITY60 + SOCIAL BONDS60 + E1

HOMICIDE70 = HOMICIDE60 + AGE70 + FEMALE LABOR FORCE
    PARTICIPATION70 + INCOME70 + %KIDS WITH ONE
    PARENT70 + MIGRATION70 + DENSITY70 + RACIAL
    COMPOSITION70 + REGION + EATING/DRINKING
    ESTABLISHMENTS70+ ALCOHOL AVAILABILITY70 + SOCIAL
    BONDS70 + E13

AGE70 = AGE60 + REGION + E14 ;
FEMALE LABOR FORCE PARTICIPATION70 = FEMALE LABOR
    FORCE PARTICIPATION60 + E15 ;
INCOME70 = INCOME60 + E16 ;
%KIDS WITH ONE PARENT70 = %KIDS WITH ONE PARENT60 + E17 ;
MIGRATION70 = MIGRATION60 + SOCIAL BONDS60 + E18 ;
DENSITY70 = DENSITY60 + E19 ;
RACIAL COMP0SITION70 = RACIAL COMPOSITION60 + E20 ;
EATING/DRINKING ESTABLISHMENTS70 = EATING/DRINKING
    ESTABLISHMENTS60 + FEMALE LABOR FORCE
    PARTICIPATION70 + E21 ;
ALCOHOL AVAILABILITY70 = ALCOHOL AVAILABILITY60 + E22 ;
SOCIAL BONDS70 = SOCIAL BONDS60 + AGE60 + INCOME70 + E23 ;

HOMICIDE80 = HOMICIDE70 + AGE80 + FEMALE LABOR FORCE
    PARTICIPATION80 + INCOME80 + %KIDS WITH ONE
    PARENT80 + MIGRATION80 + DENSITY80 + RACIAL
    COMPOSITION80 + REGION + EATING/DRINKING
    ESTABLISHMENTS80+ ALCOHOL AVAILABILITY80 + SOCIAL
    BONDS80 + E24 ;

AGE80 = AGE70 + AGE60 + E25 ;
FEMALE LABOR FORCE PARTICIPATION80 = FEMALE LABOR
    FORCE PARTICIPATION70 + E26 ;
INCOME80 = INCOME70 + E27 ;

(continued on next page)

%KIDS WITH ONE PARENT80 = %KIDS WITH ONE PARENT70 + RACIAL COMPOSITION70 + E28 ;

MIGRATION80 = MIGRATION70 + HOMICIDE70 + RACIAL COMPOSITION60 + E29;

DENSITY80 = DENSITY70 + E30 ;

RACIAL COMPOSITION80 = RACIAL COMPOSITION70 + E31 ;

EATING/DRINKING ESTABLISHMENTS80 = EATING/DRINKING ESTABLISHMENTS70 + E32 ;

ALCOHOL AVAILABILITY80 = ALCOHOL AVAILABILITY70 + E33 ;

SOCIAL BONDS80 = SOCIAL BONDS70 + MIGRATION80 + MIGRATION60 + AGE80 + %KIDS WITH ONE PARENT80 + AGE60 + E34 ;

Cities Included in Chapter 4 Analyses

AL	Burbank	Santa Rosa	FL
Birmingham	Downey	Stockton	Clearwater
Gadsden	Fresno	Torrance	Daytona Beach
Huntsville	Garden Grove	Vallejo	Fort Lauderdale
Mobile	Glendale	Whittier	Hollywood
Montgomery	Hayward		Jacksonville
Tuscaloosa	Inglewood	CO	Miami
	Long Beach	Colorado	Orlando
AZ	Los Angeles	Springs	Panama City
Phoenix	Modesto	Denver	Pensacola
Tucson	Oakland		St. Petersburg
	Palo Alto	CT	Sarasota
AR	Pasadena	Bridgeport	Tallahassee
Hot Springs	Pomona	Hartford	Tampa
Little Rock	Riverside	New Haven	West Palm
North Little Rock	Sacramento	Stamford	Beach
Pine Bluff	Salinas	Waterbury	
	San Bernadino		GA
	San Jose		Albany
CA	San Leandro	DE	Atlanta
Anaheim	San Mateo	Wilmington	Augusta
Bakersfield	Santa Ana		Columbus
Berkeley	Santa Barbara	DC	Macon
Beverly Hills	Santa Monica	Washington	Savannah

(continued on next page)

HI	**KY**	**MN**	**NM**
Honolulu	Louisville	Duluth	Albuquerque
	Owensboro	Minneapolis	
IL	Paducah	St. Paul	**NY**
Chicago			Albany
Decatur	**LA**	**MS**	Binghamton
Evanston	Baton Rouge	Jackson	Buffalo
Joliet	Lafayette	Meridian	New Rochelle
Peoria	Lake Charles		New York
Quincy	Monroe	**MO**	Niagara Falls
Rockford	New Orleans	Kansas City	Rochester
Skokie		St. Joseph	Schenectady
Springfield	**ME**	St. Louis	Syracuse
Waukegan	Portland	Springfield	Utica
			White Plains
	MD	**MT**	Yonkers
IN	Baltimore	Billings	
Anderson		Great Falls	**NC**
Evansville	**MA**		Asheville
Fort Wayne	Boston	**NB**	Burlington
Gary	Brockton	Lincoln	Charlotte
Hammond	Cambridge	Omaha	Durham
Indianapolis	Fall River		Fayetteville
Muncie	Lowell	**NV**	Greensboro
South Bend	Lynn	Las Vegas	Raleigh
Terre Haute	New Bedford	Reno	Wilmington
	Quincy		Winston-Salem
IA	Springfield	**NH**	
Cedar Rapids	Worcester	Manchester	**OH**
Davenport			Akron
Des Moines	**MI**	**NJ**	Canton
Dubuque	Ann Arbor	Bayonne	Cincinnati
Sioux City	Dearborn	Clifton	Cleveland
Waterloo	Detroit	Jersey City	Columbus
	Flint	Trenton	Dayton
KS	Kalamazoo	Newark	Hamilton
Kansas City	Lansing	Paterson	Mansfield
Topeka	Saginaw	Union City	Springfield
Wichita	Warren	Vineland	Toledo

(continued on next page)

Cities Included in Chapter 4 Analyses *(continued)*

Warren	**RI**	Beaumont	Portsmouth
Youngstown	Cranston	Dallas	Richmond
	Pawtucket	El Paso	Roanoke
OK	Providence	Fort Worth	
Lawton	Warwich	Galveston	**WA**
Tulsa		Houston	Everett
	SC	Longview	Seattle
	Anderson	Odessa	Spokane
OR	Charleston	San Antonio	Tacoma
Eugene	Columbia	Waco	Yakima
Salem	Greenville	Wichita Falls	
	Spartanburg		**WV**
PA		**UT**	Charleston
Altoona	**SD**	Ogden	Huntington
Bethlehem	Sioux Falls	Salt Lake City	
Erie			**WI**
Harrisburg	**TN**	**VA**	Green Bay
Lancaster	Chattanooga	Alexandria	Kenosha
Philadelphia	Knoxville	Danville	La Crosse
Pittsburgh	Memphis	Hampton	Madison
Reading		Lynchburg	Milwaukee
Scranton	**TX**	Newport News	Oshkosh
Wilkes-Barre	Amarillo	Norfolk	Racine
	Austin		West Allis

APPENDIX 2B

Descriptive Statistics for the Longitudinal Analyses of
Alcohol Availability and Homicide, Chapter 4

Variable	Mean	Standard deviation	Minimum	Maximum
Homicide, 1960 (per 100,000)	5.34	4.63	0.0	24.175
Median age, 1960	31.00	4.06	22.80	47.30
Female labor force participation rate, 1960	36.72	3.48	27.10	45.50
Median family income 1960	16794.83	2998.22	10196.49	33894.91
% kids living with one parent, 1960	15.98	5.81	6.10	34.20
Migration, 1960	53.26	8.26	30.30	78.30
Population density, 1960	5650.87	4058.04	561.00	40139.00
Racial composition, 1960	13.15	12.50	1.00	53.90
Region	0.32	0.47	0.0	1.0

(continued on next page)

Descriptive Statistics for the Longitudinal Analyses of
Alcohol Availability and Homicide, Chapter 4 *(continued)*

Variable	Mean	Standard deviation	Minimum	Maximum
Eating/drinking activity, 1960 (annual $ per capita)	363.30	157.81	118.922	1828.627
Alcohol availability, 1963 (per 1,000)	0.25	0.21	0.0	2.02
Social bonds, 1960	-0.97	1.12	-4.90	3.33
One parent/alcohol availability interaction, 1960	0.09	0.29	0.0	1.0
Age/alcohol availability interaction, 1960	0.07	0.26	0.0	1.0
Social bonds/alcohol availability interaction, 1960	0.06	0.24	0.0	1.0
Homicide, 1970 (per 100,000)	10.15	9.08	0.0	58.467
Median age, 1970	29.71	4.22	22.50	48.20
Female labor force participation rate, 1970	41.22	2.75	32.21	48.79
Median family income 1970	21537.17	3711.75	13554.00	45681.75
% kids living with one parent, 1970	22.19	6.79	8.40	43.40
Migration, 1970	48.77	7.56	29.50	71.40
Population density, 1970	5006.32	4190.41	682.00	44081.00
Racial composition, 1970	15.09	13.62	1.00	71.10

(continued on next page)

Descriptive Statistics for the Longitudinal Analyses of
Alcohol Availability and Homicide, Chapter 4 *(continued)*

Variable	Mean	Standard deviation	Minimum	Maximum
Region	0.32	0.47	0.0	1.0
Eating/drinking activity, 1970 (annual $ per capita)	475.22	195.15	197.00	2095.297
Alcohol availability, 1972 (per 1,000)	0.21	.13	0.0	0.91
Social bonds, 1970	-0.28	1.11	-4.864	2.74
One parent/alcohol availability interaction, 1970	0.11	0.31	0.0	1.0
Age/alcohol availability interaction, 1970	0.07	0.026	0.0	1.0
Social bonds/alcohol availability interaction, 1970	0.07	0.26	0.0	1.0
Homicide, 1980 (per 100,000)	13.76	11.44	0.0	63.43
Median age, 1980	30.56	3.36	24.50	44.20
Female labor force participation rate, 1980	45.27	2.12	38.44	51.64
Median family income 1980	21566.83	3936.60	13159.02	45942.00
% kids living with one parent, 1980	32.77	9.36	14.00	59.40
Migration, 1980	48.03	7.79	29.10	69.00
Population density, 1980	4443.83	3788.33	712.00	39709.00

(continued on next page)

Descriptive Statistics for the Longitudinal Analyses of
Alcohol Availability and Homicide, Chapter 4 *(continued)*

Variable	Mean	Standard deviation	Minimum	Maximum
Racial composition, 1980	18.57	16.44	1.00	70.77
Region	0.32	0.47	0.0	1.0
Eating/drinking activity, 1980 (annual $ per capita)	563.83	215.57	193.64	2592.98
Alcohol availability, 1982 (per 1,000)	0.20	0.11	0.02	0.80
Social bonds, 1980	0.92	1.27	-3.09	4.24
One parent/alcohol availability interaction, 1980	0.09	0.29	0.0	1.0
Age/alcohol availability interaction, 1980	0.07	0.26	0.0	1.0
Social bonds/alcohol availability interaction, 1980	0.07	0.26	0.0	1.0

Descriptive Statistics for the
Minimum Drinking Age Analysis, Chapter 5

Variable	Mean	Standard deviation	Minimum	Maximum
Primary homicide aged 15-18 (per 1,000)	0.0246	0.0187	0.0	0.123
Primary homicide aged 19-20 (per 1,000)	0.0528	0.0410	0.0	0.253
Primary homicide aged 21-24 (per 1,000)	0.0654	0.0439	0.0	0.221
Nonprimary homicide aged 15-18 (per 1,000)	0.0222	0.0271	0.0	0.280
Nonprimary homicide aged 19-20 (per 1,000)	0.0435	0.0524	0.0	0.440
Non primary homicide aged 21-24 (per 1,000)	0.0498	0.0539	0.0	0.450

(continued on next page)

Descriptive Statistics for the
Minimum Drinking Age Analysis, Chapter 5 *(continued)*

Variable	Mean	Standard deviation	Minimum	Maximum
South	0.3529	0.4785	0.0	1.0
Inequality	28.0020	7.2605	2.6	49.4
Drinking age changes	0.1936	0.3956	0.0	1.0
Total population (in thousands)	4436.7580	4660.2270	393.090	25257.080
Infant mortality (per 1,000 births)	12.6641	2.5910	7.7	29.1
Beer consumption (barrels per 1,000)	768.3791	149.3105	441.173	1250.163
Proportion nonwhite	0.1379	0.1393	0.006	0.721

REFERENCES

Abbott, E. C., and H.S. Smith. 1939. *We pointed them north: recollections of a cowpuncher.* Norman: University of Oklahoma Press.

Adams, J. 1760 (1865). "Diary, May 29, 1760," in C.F. Adams, ed., *Works of John Adams* 2:84-85.

Akers, R. L. 1973. *Deviant behavior: a social learning approach.* Belmont, Calif.: Wadsworth.

Alaniz, M. L., and R. N. Parker. 1993. "Alcohol outlet density and youth violence in the Mexican American community." Proposal funded by the California Wellness Foundation, Woodland Hills, CA.

Anselin, L. 1988. *Spatial econometrics: methods and models.* Dordrecht, The Netherlands: Kluwer Academic Publishers.

Archer, D., and R. Gartner. 1984. *Violence and crime in cross-national perspective.* New Haven: Yale University Press.

Austin, G. T. 1985. *Alcohol in western society from antiquity to 1800: a chronological history.* Santa Barbara, Calif.: ABC-Clio Information Services.

Ayers, E. L. 1984. *Vengeance and justice: crime and punishment in the 19th century American south.* New York: Oxford University Press.

Bailey, W. C. 1990. "Murder, capital punishment, and television: execution publicity and homicide rates." *American sociological review* 55:628-33.

———. 1984. "Poverty, inequality, and city homicide rates: some not so unexpected results." *Criminology* 22:531-50.

Bailey, W. C., and R. D. Peterson. 1989. "Murder and capital punishment: a monthly time series analysis of execution publicity." *American sociological review* 54:722-43.

Bentler, P. M. 1990. "Comparative fit indexes in structural models." *Psychological bulletin* 107:238-46.

Bentler, P. M., and E. J. C. Wu. 1993. *EQS/windows user's guide.* Los Angeles: BMDP Statistical Software.

Blair, W., and F. J. Meine. 1933. *Mike Fink, king of Mississippi keelboatmen.* New York: Aldine.

Blau, P. M. 1977. *Inequality and heterogeneity: a primitive theory of social structure.* New York: Free Press.

Blau, P. M., and R. M. Golden. 1986. "Metropolitan structure and criminal violence." *Sociological Quarterly* 27:15-26.

Blau, J. R., and P. M. Blau. 1982. "The cost of inequality: metropolitan structure and violent crime." *American sociological review* 47:114-29.

Blose, J. O., and H. D. Holder. 1987. "Public availability of distilled spirits: structural and reported consumption changes associated with liquor-by-the-drink." *Journal of studies on alcohol* 48:371-79.

Bowers, William J. 1984. *Legal homicide.* Boston: Northeastern University Press.

Bridenbaugh, G. 1971. *Cities in the wilderness: the first century of urban life in America, 1625-1742.* New York: Oxford University Press.

Browne, A., and K. R. Williams. 1989. "Exploring the effect of resource availability and the likelihood of female-perpetrated homicides." *Law and Society Review* 23:75-94.

Byrne, J., and R. J. Sampson. 1984. *The social ecology of crime: theory, research and public policy.* Chicago: University of Chicago Press.

Cahalan, D. 1987. *Understanding America's drinking problem: how to combat the hazards of alcohol.* San Francisco: Jossey-Bass Publishers.

Campbell, D. T., and J. C. Stanley. 1963. *Experimental and quasi-experimental designs for research.* Chicago: Rand McNally.

Campbell, R. T., E. J. Mutran, and R. N. Parker. 1986. "Longitudinal design and longitudinal analysis: a comparison of three approaches." *Research on aging* 8:480-502.

Carroll, L., and P. I. Jackson. 1983. "Inequality, opportunity, and crime rates in central cities." *Criminology* 21: 178-94.

Carsten, O. 1981. "Use of the nationwide personal transportation study to calculate exposure." *HSRI Research Review* 11:1-8.

Christiansen, B. A., M. S. Goldman, and S. A. Brown. 1985. "The differential development of alcohol expectancies may predict adult alcoholism." *Addictive Behaviors* 10:299-306.

Cliff, A. D., and J. K. Ord. 1973. *Spatial autocorrelation.* London: Pion.

Cohen, J. 1977. *Statistical power analysis for the behavioral sciences.* New York: Academic Press.

Cohen, L. E., and M. Felson. 1979. "Social change and crime rate trends: a routine activities approach." *American sociological review* 44: 588-607.

Cohen, L. E., J. Kluegal, and K. Land. 1981. "Social inequality and predatory criminal victimization: an exposition and test of a formal theory." *American sociological review* 46:505-24.

Cohen, L. E., and K. C. Land. 1987. "Age structure and crime: symmetry vs. asymmetry, and projections of crime rates through the 1990s." *American sociological review* 52:170-83.

Collins, J. J., Jr. 1989. "Alcohol and interpersonal violence: less than meets the eye" in N. A. Weiner and M. E. Wolfgang, eds., *Pathways to criminal violence.* Newbury Park, Calif.: Sage Publications, 49-67.

———. 1983. "Alcohol use and expressive interpersonal violence: a proposed explanatory model" in E. Gottheil, K. A. Druley, T. E. Sakoda, and H. M. Waxman, eds., *Alcohol, drug abuse, and aggression.* Springfield, Ill.: Charles Thomas, 5-25.

———. 1981. "Alcohol use and criminal behavior: an empirical, theoretical, and methodological overview" in J. J. Collins, Jr., editor, *Drinking and crime.* New York: Guilford Press, 288-316.

Cook, K. S., and R. M. Emerson. 1978. "Power, equity, and commitment in exchange networks." *American sociological review* 43:721-39.

Cook, K. S., K. A. Hegtvedt, and T. Yamagishi. 1987. "Structural inequality, legitimation, and reactions to inequity in exchange networks" in M. Webster and M. Foschi, eds., *Status generalization: new theory and research.* Stanford: Stanford University Press, 291-309.

Cook, P. J. 1981. "The effect of gun availability on violent crime patterns." *Annuals of the Academy of Political and Social Science* 455:63-79.

——. 1991. "The technology of personal violence" in M. Tonry, ed., *Crime and justice, a review of research.* Chicago: University of Chicago Press, 1-71.

Cook, P. J., and M. J. Moore. 1993a. "Violence reduction through restrictions on alcohol availability." *Alcohol health and research world* 17:151-56.

——. 1993b. "Economic perspectives on reducing alcohol-related violence" in S. Martin, ed., *Alcohol and interpersonal violence: multidisciplinary perspectives.* Rockville, Md.: U.S. Department of Health and Human Services, NIAAA Research Monograph #24, pp. 193-212.

Cook, P. J., and G. Tauchen. 1982. "The effect of liquor taxes on heavy drinking." *Bell journal of economics* 13:379-90.

——. 1984. "The effects of minimum drinking age legislation on youthful auto fatalities, 1970-77." *Journal of legal studies* 13:169-90.

Cook, T. D., and D. T. Campbell. 1979. *Quasi-experimentation: design and analysis issues for field settings.* Chicago: Rand McNally.

Crutchfield, R. D. 1989. "Labor stratification and violent crime." *Social Forces* 68:489-512.

Cucchiaro, S., J. Ferreira, Jr., and A. Sicherman. 1974. *The effect of 18 year old drinking age on auto accidents.* Cambridge: M.I.T., Operations Research Center.

Daly, M., and M. Wilson. 1988. *Homicide.* New York: Aldine De Gruyter.

DeFranzo, J. 1983. "Economic assistance to impoverished Americans." *Criminology* 21:119-36.

Distilled Spirits Council of the U.S. 1989. *Summary of the state laws and regulations relating to distilled spirits.* Washington, D.C.: Distilled Spirits Council of the U.S.

Dodd, J. S. 1978. "The working classes and the temperance movement in ante-bellum Boston." *Labor history* 19, 4:510-31.

Douglas, R. L., L. D. Filkins, and F. A. Clark. 1974. *The effect of lower legal drinking ages on youth crash involvement.* Ann Arbor: University of Michigan, Highway Safety Research Institute.

Dozier, E. F. 1966. "Problem drinking among American Indians: the role of sociocultural deprivation." *Quarterly journal of studies on alcohol* 27, 1:72-87.

Earle, A. M. 1913. *Home life in colonial days.* New York: Macmillan.

Elliot, D., D. Huizinga, and S. Ageton. 1985. *Explaining delinquency and drug use.* Beverly Hills, Calif.: Sage Publications.

Fagan, J. 1990. "Intoxication and aggression" in M. Torny and J. Q. Wilson, eds., *Drugs and crime,* vol. 13, Crime and Justice: A Review of Research. Chicago: University of Chicago Press, 241-320.

Federal Bureau of Investigation. 1992. *Crime in the United States 1991.* Washington, D.C.: U.S. Government Printing Office.

——— . 1987. Supplemental Homicide Report. Machine readable data files for years 1976-83.

——— . 1983. *Crime in the United States 1982.* Washington, D.C.: U.S. Government Printing Office.

——— . 1973. *Crime in the United States 1972.* Washington, D.C.: U.S. Government Printing Office.

——— . 1964. *Crime in the United States 1963.* Washington, D.C.: U.S. Government Printing Office.

Felson, R. B., and H. J. Steadman. 1983. "Situational factors in disputes leading to criminal violence." *Criminology* 21:59-74.

Ferdinand, T. 1967. "The criminal patterns of Boston since 1849." *American journal of sociology* 73:84-99.

Ferris, R., T. B. Malone, and H. Lilliefore. 1976. *A comparison of alcohol involvement in exposed and injured drivers.* Alexandria, Va.: Essex Corporation.

Gartner, R. 1990. "The victims of homicide: a temporal and cross-national comparison." *American sociological review* 55:92-106.

Gartner, R., and R. N. Parker. 1990. "Cross-national evidence on homicide and the age structure of the population." *Social forces* 69:351-72.

Gastil, R. P. 1971. "Homicide and a regional culture of violence." *American sociological review* 36:412-27.

Glaser, F. B. 1976. "Alcoholism in Pennsylvania—a bicentennial perspective." *Pennsylvania medicine,* vol. 123, pp. 12-16.

Glenn, N. 1981. "Age, birth cohorts, and drinking: an illustration of the hazards of inferring effects from cohort data." *Journal of gerontology* 36:362-69.

Goodman, R. A., J. A. Mercy, and J. C. Rosenberg. 1985. "Alcohol use and homicide victimization: an examination of racial/ethnic differences" in *Alcohol use among U.S. ethnic minorities*. Rockville, Md.: U.S. Department of Health and Human Services, Research Monograph #18, pp. 191-207.

Gorn, E. J. 1985. "'Gouge and bite, pull hair and scratch': the social significance of fighting in the southern backcountry." *American historical review* 90, 1:18-43.

Gottfredson, M.R. 1984. *Victims of crime: the dimensions of risk*. London: Her Majesty's Stationary Office, Home Office, Research Study #81.

Gottfredson, M.R., and T. Hirschi. 1990. *A general theory of crime*. Stanford: Stanford University Press.

Gove, W. R., M. Hughes, and O. R. Galle. 1979. "Overcrowding in the home: an empirical investigation of its possible consequences." *American sociological review* 44:59-80.

Greenberg, D. F., and R. C. Kessler. 1982. "The effect of arrests on crime: a multivariate panel analysis." *Social forces* 60:771-90.

Griffith, D. A. 1988. *Advance in spatial statistics*. Dordrecht, The Netherlands: Kluwer Academic Publishers.

Gruenewald, P. J., and W. R. Ponicki. 1993. "Consumption and death: dynamic constraints on the pattern of alcohol use." Berkeley, Calif.: Prevention Research Center, #PG1103.

Gruenewald, P. J., W. R. Ponicki, and H. D. Holder. 1993. "The relationship of outlet densities to alcohol consumption: a time series cross-sectional analysis." *Alcoholism: clinical and experimental* 17:38-47.

Hackney, S. 1968. "Southern violence" in H. D. Graham and T. R. Gurr, eds., *Violence in America*. New York: Signet, 479-500.

Hagan, J. 1989. *Structural criminology*. New Brunswick: Rutgers University Press.

Hammock, G. S., and D. R. Richardson. 1993. "Blaming drunk victims: is it a just world or sex role violation?" *Journal of applied social psychology* 23:1574-86.

Hawley, A. 1950. *Human ecology: a theory of community structure*. New York: Ronald.

Heath, D. B. 1985. "American Indians and alcohol: epidemiological and sociocultural relevance" in *Alcohol use among U.S. ethnic minorities*. HHS Research Monograph 18, pp. 207-22.

Hindelang, M., M. Gottfredson, and J. Garofalo. 1978. *Victims of personal crime: an empirical foundation for a theory of personal victimization*. Cambridge, Mass.: Ballinger.

Hines, W. 1828. "An address, delivered at the Methodist chapel," Norwitch, Conn.

Hirschi, T. 1969. *Causes of delinquency*. Berkeley: University of California Press.

Hirschi, T., and M. Gottfredson. 1983. "Age and the explanation of crime." *American Journal of Sociology* 89:552-84.

Holder, H.D. 1989a. "Prevention of Alcohol Related Problems." *Alcohol Health and Research World* 13:339-42.

———. 1989b. "Drinking, alcohol availability, and injuries: a systems model of complex relationships" in N. Giesbrecht, R. Gonzalez, M. Grant, E. Osterberg, R. Room, I. Rootman, and L. Towle, eds., *Drinking and casualties: accidents, poisonings, and violence in an international perspective*. London: Associated Book Publishers, 133-48.

Holder, H. D., and A. C. Wagenaar. 1990. "Effects of the elimination of a state monopoly on distilled spirits' retail sales: a time series analysis of Iowa." *British journal of addiction* 85:1615-25.

House, J. S. 1981. "Social structure and personality" in M. Rosenberg and R. Turner, eds., *Social psychology: sociological perspectives*. New York: Basic Books, 525-61.

Huff-Corzine, L., J. Corzine, and D. Moore. 1991. "Deadly connections: culture, poverty, and the direction of lethal violence." *Social forces* 69:715-32.

———. 1986. "Southern exposure: deciphering the south's influence on homicide rates." *Social forces* 64:906-24.

Huggins, P. 1971. *The South Carolina dispensary: a bottle collector's guide and history of the system*. Columbia, S.C.: Sandlapper Press.

Hunt, G. 1983. "Spirits of the colonial economy: part one" in *New directions in the study of alcohol*. Group Members Booklet # 5, pp. 34-52.

Jackson, P. I. 1984. "Opportunity and crime: a function of city size." *Social science review* 68:172-93.

Jackson, P. I., and L. Carroll. 1981. "Race and the war on crime." *American sociological review* 46:290-305.

Janes, K., and P. J. Gruenewald. 1991. "The role of formal law in alcohol control systems: a comparison among states." *American journal of drugs and alcohol abuse* 17:199-214.

Jasso, G. 1990. "Principle of theoretical analysis." *Sociological theory* 8:123-59.

Kantor, G. K., and M. A. Straus. 1987. "The 'drunken bum' theory of wife beating." *Social problems* 34:213-31.

Katz, J. 1988. *Seductions of crime.* New York: Basic Books.

Katz, P. C. 1986. *The brewing industry in the United States: the brewers almanac.* Washington, D.C.: Beer Institute.

Klein, R. M. 1976. "A nation of moonshiners." *Natural history* 85, 1 (January): 23-31.

Krohn, M. D. 1991. "Control and deterrence theories" in J. Sheley, ed., *Criminology: a contemporary handbook.* Belmont, Calif.: Wadsworth, 295-314.

Krohn, M. D., and J. Massey. 1980. "Social control and delinquent behavior: an examination of the elements of the social bond." *Sociological Quarterly* 21: 529-43.

Land, Kenneth C., Patricia L. McCall, and Lawrence E. Cohen. 1990. "Structural covariates of homicide rates: are there invariances across time and social space?" *American journal of sociology* 95:922-63.

Lauretsen, J. L., R. Sampson, and J. H. Laub. 1991. "The link between offending and victimization among adolescents." *Criminology* 29:265-92.

Leigh, B. C. 1989. "In search of the seven dwarves: issues of measurement and meaning in alcohol expectancies research." *Psychological Bulletin* 105:361-73.

Lenke, L. 1990. *Alcohol and criminal violence: time series analysis in a comparative perspective.* Stockholm: Almqvist and Wiksell.

Leonard, K. E. 1989. "The impact of explicit aggressive and implicit nonaggressive cues on aggression in intoxicated and sober males." *Personality and social psychology bulletin* 15:390-400.

Levine, H. G. 1984. "The alcohol problem in America: from temperance to alcoholism." *British journal of addiction* 79:109-19.

——— . 1983. "The good creature of God and the demon rum: colonial Americans and 19th century ideas about alcohol, crime, and accidents" in *Alcohol and disinhibition: nature and meaning of the link.* Proceedings of a conference, February 11-13, 1981. Berkeley/Oakland, Calif. Robin Room and Gary Collins, eds. Rockville, Md.: HHS, NIAAA.

Lindqvist, P. 1986. "Criminal homicide in northern Sweden 1970-81: alcohol intoxication, alcohol abuse, and mental disease." *International journal of law and psychiatry* 8:19-37.

Liska, A., and M. D. Reed. 1985. "Ties to conventional institutions and delinquency: estimating reciprocal effects." *American sociological review* 50:547-60.

Loftin, C. K., and R. H. Hill. 1974. "Regional subculture and homicide." *American sociological review* 39:714-24.

Loftin, C. K., and D. McDowall. 1984. "The deterrent effects of the Florida firearm law." *Journal of criminal law and criminology* 75:250-59.

——— . 1981. "One with a gun gets you two: mandatory sentencing and firearms violence in Detroit." *The annals of the academy of political and social science* 455:150-81.

Loftin, C. K., and R. N. Parker. 1985. "An errors-in-variables model of the effect of poverty on urban homicide rates." *Criminology* 23:269-87.

Loftin, C. K., and S. Ward. 1983. "A spatial autocorrelation model of the effects of population density on fertility." *American sociological review* 48:121-28.

Loftin, C. K., D. McDowall, and B. Wiersema. 1992. "A comparative study of the preventive effects of mandatory sentencing laws for gun crimes." *Journal of criminal law and criminology* 83:378-94.

Luckenbill, D. F. 1977. "Criminal homicide as a situated transaction." *Social problems* 25:176-86.

MacAndrews, C., and R. Edgerton. 1969. *Drunken comportment, a social explanation.* New York: Aldine.

Maddala, G. S. 1971. "The use of variance components models in pooling cross section and time series data." *Econometrica,* 39:341-58.

Madsen, W., and C. Madsen. 1969. "The cultural structure of Mexican drinking behavior." *Journal of studies on alcohol* 30:701-18.

Males, M. A. 1986. "The minimum purchase age for alcohol and young-driver fatal crashes: a longterm view." *Journal of legal studies* 15:181-217.

Marshall, M., ed. 1979. *Beliefs, behaviors, & alcoholic beverages: a cross-cultural survey.* Ann Arbor: University of Michigan Press.

Mather, C. 1708. *Sober considerations.* Boston.

Maxfield, M. G. 1987. "Lifestyle and routine activity theories of crime: empirical studies of victimization, delinquency, and offender decision making." *Journal of quantitative criminology* 3:275-81.

Maxwell, B., and Jacobson, M. 1989. *Marketing disease to Hispanics.* Washington, D.C.: Center for Science in the Public Interest.

Messner, S. F. 1989. "Economic discrimination and societal homicide rates: further evidence of the cost of inequality." *American sociological review* 54:597-611.

———. 1983a. "Regional and racial effects on the urban homicide rate: the subculture of violence revisited." *American journal of sociology* 88, 997-1007.

———. 1983b. "Regional differences in the economic correlates of the urban homicide rates: some evidence on the importance of context." *Criminology* 21, 477-88.

———. 1982 "Poverty, inequality, and the urban homicide rate." *Criminology* 20:103-14.

Messner, S. F., and R. J. Sampson. 1991. "The sex ratio, family disruption, and rates of violent crime: the paradox of demographic structure." *Social forces* 69:693-714.

Messner, S. F., and K. Tardiff. 1986. "Economic inequality and levels of homicide: an analysis of urban neighborhoods." *Criminology* 24:297-318.

———. 1985. "The social ecology of urban homicide: an application of the routine activities approach." *Criminology* 23: 241-67.

Miethe, T. D., M. C. Stafford, and J. S. Long. 1987. "Social differentiation in criminal victimization: a test of routine activities/lifestyle theories." *American sociological review* 52:184-94.

Murdock, D., and R. O. Pihl. 1988. "The influence of beverage type of aggression in males in the natural setting." *Aggressive behavior* 14:325-36.

Murdoch, D., R. O. Pihl, and D. Ross. 1990. "Alcohol and crimes of violence." *International journal of the addictions* 25:1059-75.

National Center for Health Statistics. 1977-84. *Vital Statistics of the U.S.* Vol. 2. Washington, D.C.: U.S. Government Printing Office.

National Committee for Injury Prevention and Control. 1989. *Injury prevention: meeting the challenge.* American Journal of Preventive Medicine 5, Supplement.

National Institute of Alcohol Abuse and Alcoholism (NIAAA). 1993. "Research on relationships between alcohol and violence." Program Announcement PA-93-095. Rockville, Md.: U.S. Department of Health and Human Services.

———. 1987. *Alcohol and Health.* Rockville, Md.: NIAAA.

———. 1985. "U.S. Apparent Consumption of Alcoholic Beverages based on State Sales, Taxation, or Receipt Data" in *U.S. Alcohol Epidemiological Data Reference Manual.* Rockville, Md.: NIAAA.

National Research Council. 1993. *Understanding and preventing violence.* A. J. Reiss, Jr., and J. A. Roth, eds. Washington, D.C.: National Academy Press.

Nerlove, M. 1971. "A note on error components models." *Econometrica* 46:383-96.

Office of Substance Abuse Prevention. 1992. "Alcohol-related injuries: the hurt and the harm." Prepared for the Secretary's National Conference on Alcohol-Related Injuries, March 1992. Washington, D.C.

O'Malley, P. M., and A. C. Wagenaar. 1991. "Effects of minimum drinking age laws on alcohol use, related behaviors, and traffic crash involvement among American youth: 1976-87." *Journal of studies on alcohol* 52:478-91.

Ornstein, S. I., and D. M. Hanssens. 1985. "Alcohol control laws and the consumption of distilled spirits and beer." *Journal of consumer research* 12: 200-213.

Parker, R. N. 1994a. "Violent crime" in Joseph F. Sheley, ed., *Criminology: a contemporary handbook,* 2nd edition. Belmont, Calif.: Wadsworth, 143-60.

———. 1994b. "Bringing 'booze' back in: the relationship between alcohol and homicide." *Journal of Research in Crime and Delinquency* 34 (In press).

————. 1993a. "Alcohol and theories of homicide" in F. Adler and W. Laufer, eds., *Advances in criminological theory*, vol. 4. New Brunswick, N.J.: Transaction Publishers, 113-42.

————. 1993b. "The effects of context on alcohol and violence." *Alcohol health and research world* 17:117-22.

————. 1992a. "Alcohol, homicide and cultural context: a cross national analysis of gender specific homicide victimization." Toronto: presented at the 18th annual Alcohol Epidemiological Symposium.

————. 1992b. "Bringing 'booze' back in: the relationship between alcohol and homicide." Pittsburgh: presented at the annual meeting of the American Sociological Association.

————. 1991. "Minimum drinking age and youth homicide: a preliminary empirical assessment." San Francisco: presented at the annual meeting of the American Society of Criminology.

————. 1989. "Poverty, Subculture of Violence, and Type of Homicide." *Social forces* 67:983-1007.

————. 1985. "Aggregation, ratio variables and measurement problems in criminological research." *Journal of quantitative criminology* 1:269-80.

Parker, R. N., and M. D. Smith. 1979. "Deterrence, poverty, and type of homicide." *American journal of sociology* 85:614-24

Parker, R. N., and A. M. Toth. 1990. "Family, intimacy, and homicide: a macro-social approach." *Violence and victims* 5:195-210.

Parks, E. L. 1976. "From constabulary to police society: implications for social control" in *Whose law? whose order?* Chambliss, William J., and Milton Mankoff, eds. New York: John Wiley, 129-47.

Pernanen, K. 1991. *Alcohol in human violence.* New York: Guilford Press.

————. 1981. "Theoretical aspects of the relationship between alcohol use and crime" in J. J. Collins, Jr., ed., *Drinking and crime.* New York: Guilford Press, 1-69.

————. 1976. "Alcohol and crimes of violence" in B. Kissin and H. Begleiter, eds., *The biology of alcoholism: social aspects of alcoholism.* New York: Plenum Press, 351-444.

Pihl, R. O., J. B. Peterson, and M. A. Lau. 1993. "A biosocial model of the alcohol-aggression relationship." *Journal of studies on alcohol,* Supplement #11, September, 128-39.

Ponicki, W. 1990. "The price and income elasticies of the demand for alcohol: a review of the literature." Berkeley, Calif.: Prevention Research Center, #WP801.

Radelet, M. L. 1981. "Racial characteristics and the imposition of the death penalty." *American sociological review* 46:918-27.

Redfield, H. V. 1880. *Homicide north and south: being a comparative view of crimes against the person in the several parts of the United States.* Philadelphia: J. B. Lippincott.

Rogers, R. G. 1992. "Living and dying in the USA: sociodemographic determinants of death among blacks and whites." *Demography* 29:287-304.

Roizen, J. 1981. "Alcohol and Criminal Behavior among African-Americans: The Case for Research on Special Populations" in J. J. Collins, Jr., ed., *Drinking and Crime.* New York: Guilford Press, 207-52.

Room, R. 1989. "Responses to alcohol-related problems in an international perspective: characterizing and explaining cultural wetness and dryness." Paper presented at La ricera Italiana sulle bevande alcoiche nel confronto internazionale, Santo Stefano Belbo, Italy, September.

———. 1983. "Region and Urbanization as Factors in Drinking Practices and Problems" in B. Kissin and H. Begleiter, eds., *The Pathogenesis of Alcoholism: Psychological Factors.* Volume 6, *The Biology of Alcoholism* series. New York: Plenum Press, 555-604.

———. 1972. "Relations between ethnic and cross-national comparisons." *Drinking and Drug Practices Surveyor* 5:12.

Room, R., and G. Collins, eds. 1983. *Alcohol and Disinhibition: Nature and Meaning of the Link.* Washington, D.C.: National Institute on Alcohol Abuse and Alcoholism, Research Monograph #12.

Rorabaugh, W. J. 1979. *The alcoholic republic: an American tradition.* New York: Oxford University Press.

Rosenfeld, R. 1986. "Urban crime rates: effects of inequality, welfare dependency, region, and race" in J. M. Byrne and R. J. Sampson, eds., *The social ecology of crime.* New York: Springer-Verlag, 116-30.

Saffer, H., and M. Grossman. 1987. "Drinking age laws and highway mortality rates: cause and effect." *Economic inquiry* 25:403-17.

Saltz, R. F. 1993. "The introduction of dram shop legislation in the United States and the advent of server training." *Addiction* 88(supplement) 95S-103S.

———. 1987. "The role of bars and restaurants in preventing alcohol-impaired driving: an evaluation of server intervention." *Evaluation and the health professions* 10:5-27.

———. 1986. "Server intervention: will it work?" *Alcohol health and research world* 10:12-19.

Saltz, R. F., and D. Elandt. 1986, Spring. "College student drinking studies, 1976-1985." *Contemporary drug problems* 13(1):117-59.

Saltz, R. F., and M. Hennessy. 1990a. "The efficacy of 'responsible beverage service' programs in reducing intoxication." Berkeley, Calif.: Prevention Research Center, #RS801.

———. 1990b. "Reducing intoxication in commercial establishments: an evaluation of responsible beverage service practices." Berkeley, Calif.: Prevention Research Center, #RS804.

Sampson, R. J. 1987. "Urban African-American violence: the effect of male joblessness and family disruption." *American journal of sociology* 93:348-82.

———. 1985. "Race and criminal violence: a demographically dissaggre-gated analysis of urban homicide." *Crime and delinquency* 31:47-82.

Sampson, R. J., and J. D. Wooldredge. 1987. "Linking the micro- and macro-level dimensions of lifestyle, routine activity and opportunity models of predatory victimization." *Journal of quantitative criminology* 3:371-93.

Samuels, F.G. 1976. *The Negro Tavern: A Microcosm of Slum Life.* San Francisco: R&E Research Associates.

Sherman, L. W., P. R. Gartin, and M. E. Buerger. 1989. "Hot spots of preda-tory crime: routine activities and the criminology of place." *Criminology* 27-56.

Silverman, R. A., and L. W. Kennedy. 1987. "Relational distance and homi-cide: the role of the stranger." *Journal of criminal law and criminology* 78: 272-308.

Skog, O.-J. 1986. "Trends in alcohol consumption and violent deaths." *British journal of addiction* 81: 365-79.

Skogan, W. G. 1978. "Weapon use in robbery" in J. A. Inciardi and A. E. Pottieger, eds., *Violent crime: historical and contemporary issues.* Beverly Hills, Calif.: Sage Publications, 61-74.

Skvoretz, J. 1983. "Salience, heterogeneity, and consolidation of parameters: civilizing Blau's primitive theory." *American sociological review* 48:360-75.

Smart, R. G. 1977. "The relationship of availability of alcohol beverages to per capita consumption and alcoholism rates." *Journal of studies on alcohol* 38:891-96.

Smith, D. A., and G. R. Jarjoura. 1988. "Social structure and criminal victimizations." *Journal of research in crime and delinquency* 25:27-52.

Smith, M. D., and R. N. Parker. 1980. "Type of homicide and variation in regional rates." *Social forces* 59:136-47.

South, S. J., and S. F. Messner. 1986. "Structural determinants of intergroup association: interracial marriage and crime." *American journal of sociology* 91:1409-30.

Sparrow, M., R. Brazeau, H. Collins, and R.A. Morrison. 1989. *Alcoholic beverage taxation and control policies: an international survey*, 7th ed. Ottawa: Brewers Association of Canada.

Steele, C., and R. Josephs. 1990. "Alcohol myopia: its prized and dangerous effects." *American psychologist* 45:921-33.

Steffensmeier, D., and E. Allan. 1991. "Gender, age, and crime" in J. Sheley, ed., *Criminology: a contemporary handbook*. Belmont, Calif.: Wadsworth, 67-94.

Steffensmeier, D., and M. Harer. 1987. "Is the crime rate really falling? an aging U.S. population and its impact on the nation's crime rate." *Journal of research in crime and delinquency* 24:23-48.

Stets, J. E. 1990. "Verbal and Physical Aggression in Marriage." *Journal of marriage and the family* 43:721-32.

Stimson, J. A. 1985. "Regression in space and time: a statistical essay." *American journal of political science* 29:915-47.

Taylor, S., and K. Leonard. 1983. "Alcohol and human physical aggression" in R. Green and E. Donnerstein, eds., *Aggression: theoretical and empirical reviews*, vol. 2, *Issues in Research*. New York: Academic Press.

Thornberry, T. P. 1987. "Toward an interactional theory of delinquency." *Criminology* 25:863-92.

Treno, A. J., and R. N. Parker. 1993. "U.S. alcohol consumption by beverage type, 1950-86: a social and economic time series analysis." Berkeley, Calif.: Prevention Research Center, #AT1103.

Treno, A. J., R. N. Parker, and H. D. Holder. 1993. "Understanding U.S. alcohol consumption with social and economic factors: a multivariate time series analysis." *Journal of studies on alcohol* 54:146-56.

Treno, A. J., T. M. Nephew, W. R. Ponicki, and P. J. Gruenewald. 1993. "Alcohol beverage price spectra: opportunities for substitution." *Alcoholism: clinical and experimental* 17:675-80.

Turner, F. J. 1894. "The significance of the frontier in American history" in *American historical association annual report for the year 1893*. Washington, D.C.: American Historical Association, 197-227

Twain, M. 1883. *Life on the Mississippi. with more than 300 illustrations* (sold by subscription only). Boston: J.R. Osgood.

Tyrrell, I. R. 1982. "Drink and temperance in the ante-bellum south: an overview and interpretation." *Journal of southern history* 68, 4: 485-510.

U.S. Bureau of the Census. 1977-80, 1982-84. *Current population reports.* Series P-25. Washington, D.C.: U.S. Government Printing Office.

———. 1983a. *Census of the population.* Vol. 1. Washington, D.C.: U.S. Government Printing Office.

———. 1983b. *City and county data book consolidated file.* Machine readable data file. Washington, D.C.: U.S. Department of Commerce.

———. 1982. *Census of business, retail trade.* Washington, D.C.: U.S. Government Printing Office.

———. 1977. *Current population reports.* Series P-60. Washington, D.C.: U.S. Government Printing Office.

———. 1974. *Census of business, retail trade.* Washington, D.C.: U.S. Government Printing Office.

———. 1963. *Census of business.* Washington, D.C.: U.S. Government Printing Office.

U.S. Bureau of Justice Statistics. 1992. *Criminal Victimization in the U.S., 1991.* Washington, D.C.: U.S. Government Printing Office.

Vingilis, E. R., and K. DeGenova. 1984. "Youth and the forbidden fruit: experiences with changes in the legal drinking age in North America." *Journal of criminal justice* 12:161-72.

Wagenaar, A. C. 1983. *Alcohol, Young Drivers, and Traffic Accidents: Effects of Minimum-Age Laws.* Lexington, Mass.: D.C. Heath.

Waller, J. A., E. M. King, G. Nielson, and H. W. Turkel. 1970. "Alcohol and other factors in California highway fatalities" in *Proceedings of the 11th annual meeting of the American association for automotive medicine.* Springfield, Ill.: Charles C. Thomas.

Walton, H., Jr. 1970. "Another Force for Disenfranchisement: Blacks and the Prohibitionists in Tennessee." *Journal of human relations* 18, 1:728-38.

Weber, M. 1898 (1958). *The Protestant ethic and the spirit of capitalism.* New York: Charles Scribner's Sons, translated by T. Parsons.

Welte, J. W., and E. L. Abel. 1989. "Homicide: drinking by the victim." *Journal of studies on alcohol* 50:197-201.

West, D., and D. Farrington. 1977. *The delinquent way of life.* London: Heinemann.

White, H. R., R. J. Pandina, and R. L. LaGrange. 1987. "Longitudinal predictors of serious substance use and delinquency." *Criminology* 25:715-40.

Whitehead, P. C., J. Craig, N. Langford, C. MacArthur, B. Stanton, and R. G. Ferrence. 1975. "Collision behavior of young drivers: impact of the change in age of majority." *Journal of studies on alcohol* 36:1208-23.

Widom, C. S. 1989. "Does violence breed violence? a critical examination of the literature." *Psychological bulletin* 106:3-28

Wilbanks, W. 1984. *Murder in Miami.* Lantham, Md.: University Press of America.

Williams, G. D., F. S. Stinson, D. Clem, and J. Noble. 1992. *Surveillance report #23: apparent per capita alcohol consumption: national, state, and regional trends, 1977-1990.* Rockville, Md.: NIAAA.

Williams, K. R. 1984. "Economic sources of homicide: reestimating the effects of poverty and inequality." *American sociological review* 49:283-89.

Williams, K. R., and R. L. Flewelling. 1988. "The social production of criminal homicide: a comparative study of disaggregated rates in American cities." *American sociological review* 53, 421-31.

———. 1987. "Family, acquaintance, and stranger homicides: alternative procedures for rate calculations." *Criminology* 25:543-60.

Wilson, W. J. 1987. *The truly disadvantaged: the inner city, the underclass, and public policy.* Chicago: University of Chicago Press.

Winkler, A. M. 1968. "Drinking on the American frontier." *Journal of studies on alcohol* 29, 2:413-45.

Wittman, F. D., and M. E. Hilton. 1987. "Uses of planning and zoning ordinances to regulate alcohol outlets in California cities," 377-66, in H. D. Holder, ed., *Control issues in alcohol abuse prevention: strategies for states and communities*. Greenwich, Conn.: JAI Press.

Wolfgang, M. E. 1958. *Patterns in criminal homicide*. Philadelphia: University of Pennsylvania Press.

Zimring, F. 1972. "The medium is the message: firearm caliber as a determinant of death from assault." *Journal of legal studies* 1:97-123.

INDEX

A

active constraint, 34-41, 47, 48, 49, 52-53, 70, 107
African-Americans, 32, 40, 47, 74, 86
  proportion of population, 61
African slaves, 9, 11, 13-14, 21
age, 59, 92, 94, 95, 98, 121
  measure of, 68, 75
  minimum, to purchase alcohol legally (*see* minimum age of purchase)
alcohol
  abuse, 2, 7
  ancient history of, 1
  availability of (*see* alcohol availability)
  consumption of (*see* alcohol consumption)
  control of (*see* alcohol control policy)
  effects of, 37-38
  links to homicide, 2, 3, 26-28, 31-44, 55, 101, 118
    cultural origins of, 5-7

empirical studies on, 4
historical background of, 1-25
macro-level approach, 28-33, 55
micro-level approach, xiv-xv
offenders and, 40
poverty and, 51
regulation and taxation, xiv, 19-22, 26
routine behavior related to, 128
treatment resources, 91
victimization and, 40
violence and, xi, 2, 3, 22, 41, 116, 124, 132
alcoholism, 22
alcohol-related automobile crashes. *See* drunk driving, crashes
alcohol availability, 41, 44, 59, 67, 70, 85, 87, 89, 90, 94, 100, 106
  in cities, 73, 77
  measure of, 60, 74
  state monopoly controls on, 62, 124

class differences, 15
    power relations and crime, 50-
        52
    violence and, 11
collective violence. *See* violence,
    collective
colonial period in U.S. history, 7-9
constraint. *See* active constraint
    and passive constraint
control theory. *See* social bonds *or*
    social control approach
County and City Data Book,
    Consolidated File, 73
crime
    class-based power relations
        and, 59, 61
    emotions and, 49-50
    self-control and, 53
criminological theory, 27, 48-53,
    118
crowding, 90
Current Population Reports, P-25,
    76
Current Population Reports, P-60,
    75

D

Dade County, Florida, 38-41
data availability, 57
deterrence theory, 4
deviance, 47-48
disinhibition, 18, 20-21, 34, 62
disinhibition, selective, 33-41, 49,
    53-54, 55, 57, 67, 70, 71, 83,
    85, 90, 92, 100, 106, 107,
    110, 116, 131
disorganization. *See* social bonds
dram shop liability, 130

Drinking and Crime (Collins), x
drinking
    history over life cycle, 69, 109
    early vs. late onset, 69, 109, 110
    buying and accepting drinks,
        14-15
drunk driving, 25
    crashes, 104
dueling, 13-14, 21

E

economic deprivation, 23
    indicators of, 61-62
economic deprivation approach,
    44, 46-47, 58
economic hierarchy, 14
economic inequality, 86, 108
emotions, crime and. *See* crime,
    emotions and
employed adults, 48, 60
EQS for Windows, 66, 79
ethnic tensions, violence and, 11,
    13
    changes in, 15

F

Federal Bureau of Investigation, 57
female labor force participation,
    59, 66, 69, 74, 77, 78, 84, 85,
    86, 89, 90, 92, 97
floor effects, 135

G

General Theory of Crime, A
    (Gottfredson and Hirschi),
    48, 52-53

M

Maine, alcohol-related crashes in, 104
male honor, 12-15, 21
Massachusetts, alcohol-related crashes in, 104
Mexican-Americans, targeted alcohol promotion to, 125
Michigan, alcohol-related crashes in, 104
migration, 61, 80, 84-85, 92, 97
measure of, 74
minimum age of purchase, ix, 25, 68-76, 103-105, 108
decreases in, 104
homicide and
potential gender effect, 120-22
potential race/ethnicity effect, 120-22
increases in, 104-105
indicator of change in, 75-76
traffic fatalities and, 104-105
minimum age of purchase, policy impact study, 68-76, 102-17, 135-45
design of, 71-72, 107-10
measures in, 75-76
results of, 102-17
sources of data for, 75-76
use of pooled cross-sectional time series models, 135, 140-45
floor effects in models, 135, 145
Minnesota, raising of minimum age of purchase in, 104, 108
modeling, multi-equation, 43
moonshiners, 17-18

multicolinearity, 67
multiple-perspective models, 68
Murder in Miami (Wilbanks), 44-48

N

National Crime Victimization Survey, 87
National Institute on Alcohol Abuse and Alcoholism (NIAAA), x, xi
National Science Foundation (NSF), xi
Native Americans, 9-11, 21
New York (state), raising minimum age of purchase in, 108
non-primary homicide. *See* homicide, non-primary
northern U.S., 15

O

Ohio, raising minimum age of purchase in, 108
Ontario, Canada, alcohol-related crashes in, 104

P

passive constraint, 34-41
Pernanen, Kai, x-xi
personality, 29
police powers, growth of, 19
policy. *See* public policy
policy based analysis, 30
pooling, impact of, 135, 140-45

population, total, 71, 108, 109,
    115, 116
  measures of, 76
population density, 62, 74
poverty, 44, 67, 77, 86, 87, 89, 90,
    100, 114, 116, 121
  alcohol consumption and, 43
  family disruption and, 86
  homicide and, 46-47
  measure of, 68, 71, 75
  See also economic deprivation
    approach
poverty-line measure, 61
Prevention Research Center, x, xi,
    xii
primary homicide. See homicide,
    primary
Prohibition, 5, 6, 7, 18, 22
public policy, 4, 7, 25, 42, 55, 101,
    102-107, 118, 129-33
  alcohol availability and, 129-
    30
  research for, 27-28
Puritans, 7-9

Q

quasi-experimental design, 103,
    105

R

racial composition, 71, 80, 84-85,
    86, 89, 90, 92, 94, 97, 108,
    114, 116
  measure of, 74, 76
racial tensions and violence. See
    ethnic tensions, violence
    and

regulation of alcohol serving out-
    lets, 129-31
  density and location, 129-30
regulatory agencies, 19
research, further studies, 118-33
research strategies, 64-89
responsible beverage service,
    130
retail activity of eating and drink-
    ing establishments, 60, 66,
    74, 90
"righteous slaughter," 49
rioting, Los Angeles in 1992, 51
rough-and-tumble, or gouging, 13-
    15, 21
routine activities, 82, 92
routine activities or lifestyles
    approach, 23, 44-46, 58, 59-
    60, 67, 77, 126
  violence and, 45

S

school enrollment, 48, 60
Seductions of Crime (Katz), 25,
    48-50
selective disinhibition. See disin-
    hibition, selective
self-control, 52-53
server intervention, 130
single-parent households, 46-47,
    61, 68, 74, 87, 98
slave trade, 8
social bonds, 23, 52-53, 75, 77, 80,
    92, 97
social bonds or social control
    approach, 25, 44, 47-48, 58
social bonds, measure of, 60-61,
    67, 74